GHOSTING

GHOSTING
A WIDOW'S VOYAGE OUT

A MEMOIR

Barbara Lazear Ascher

PUSHCART

ISBN: 978-0-9600977-6-0

Pushcart Press
P.O. Box 380
Wainscott, New York 11975

Distributed by W.W. Norton Co.
500 Fifth Avenue
New York, New York 10110

Designed by Mary Kornblum

PRINTED IN THE UNITED STATES OF AMERICA

Ghost, v; To make headway slowly when there appears to be no wind.

The Sailing Dictionary

A RIDDLE

What's at the end of a great love affair?
A survivor in love with a ghost.

Prologue

MY FAVORITE MOMENTS UNDER SAIL were when we were ghosting, making slow, silent progress across the water in a breeze so slight it seemed it wasn't there at all.

Unlike occasions when the wind died and the sail's flapping protests demanded action, ghosting was unaccompanied by orders from the cockpit to lower and furl, to turn on the engine. There was no rush of diesel exhaust and churning water. Ghosting required none of that scurrying and racket. It called upon nothing other than patience as we glided homeward with the ease of a swan.

This tended to occur late in the day, that time when the setting sun spills itself across the water. An offering. It bestowed a sense of oneness. Sailor and vessel, breeze and breath, sea and sky. Whatever conversation we'd been having, and we were always having one, would cease.

But of course, it couldn't last. The wind would return, we would adjust the sail to receive it, the chatter would resume. Speed with its sense of urgency, its assurance of a quicker arrival at our destination would re-enter our life leaving me disappointed. I had a tendency to long for what had been and this change in conditions was no exception.

Ghosting is defined by the apparent absence of an element vital to the enterprise. Appearance isn't a reliable measure of reality. A phantom breeze can fill a sail.

Entwined

AND A PHANTOM CELL CAN CHANGE A LIFE.

That summer, did our bodies know what our conscious minds did not? Alone, we clung to one another during our six weeks aboard the small boat. The children — Bob's three from his marriage to Carol, Elizabeth (Lizzie,) Ellen and Steven were ashore with children of their own. Our daughter Rebecca was at work in New York.

When we swam from the boat I didn't go ashore for my usual, solitary walk. Nor did he take sponge in hand to wash the hull. We stayed close, reaching out mid-stroke to touch the others foot, leg, arm. Lying in the cockpit, drying in the sun, we pressed against each other's briny skin.

In sleep, we remained entwined. One dawn we awakened to discover our lips still touching, holding last night's kiss.

We rejoiced in Nantucket Harbor as the full moon rose, the sun set and Brandt Point Light moaned. We celebrated dinners ashore or on board, naked swims through foggy nights, quiet anchorage in Hadley's Harbor. There was peace that summer, a quality sporadic in the past when I elbowed against the cramped space. That summer, I didn't want to be somewhere else, doing something else.

On Labor Day eve, our last night on board when we sat down to dinner, Bob lifted his glass and said, "This has been the best summer of my life."

That Fall

"IT WAS THE CHICKEN SANDWICH," he said, back in the car following another of many crucial pit stops on the drive home. "You drive." I thought but did not say, you must be very, very sick if you want me to drive. He had never been able to relax with me behind the wheel. His right foot would press down on an invisible brake, and if his eyes were closed in an attempted nap, they would snap open when I changed lanes.

He had seemed fine that morning as we unloaded the boat, hauling lines, foul weather gear, toolboxes, winch handles to the shipyard's storage bin. We'd stood together when the job was done, marveling at how when no longer weighed down by the necessities of life aboard, the boat rose and bobbed above the waterline. "She looks as light as a duck," we noted as we always did.

But he was no longer fine. Severe nausea set in after we'd shared a chicken sandwich at our favorite Rhode Island diner. I'd found it to be perfect. Toasted white bread, the right amount of may-onnaise binding but not drowning the chopped meat and celery, sliced just so on the diagonal, one half placed on each white plate. The matronly waitress called each of us, "Hon."

"But we split the sandwich and I'm fine."

"Still," he said.

There were to be many more stops before we drove across the Triboro Bridge, that moment between Queens and the city when Bob's annual gloom enveloped like the smog symbolizing the end of his idyll. Back to work. Back to tie and jacket. Back to life by the clock.

Through the fall, he became sicker but resisted tests. "The doctor will just say..." Typical. Doctors always seem to "know" what the other doctor will say. No need to go to one. We continued our usual lives in spite of his constant and increasing intestinal pain. Another common characteristic of physicians — they carry on. Five days a week he saw his psychiatric patients and I went into my office to tackle the day's writing. On weekends he'd attempt to play tennis with his "tennis buddies."

At night in bed, he asked me to press my stomach against his back to warm it where additional pain had travelled. At meals, he ate smaller and smaller amounts. I attributed it to age. Why would a seventy-seven -year-old require the calorie intake of the young, the growing, the active?

I urged him to go to an infectious disease doctor I'd once consulted for a stomach ailment following a writing assignment in a suspect locale. "It's quick," I told him. "He sticks his finger up your butt, then looks at your poop under a microscope and gives you the diagnosis while you're still there. No taking those nasty specimens to a lab."

"Far too many positive diagnoses," David, our internist and Bob's trusted colleague and longtime friend grumbled when Bob informed him of my suggestion. The world and those therein rarely rose to David's standards. That's why we entrusted our bodies to him.

Nonetheless, Bob agreed to my urging. To make it easier to fit the appointment in between patients, to get around his claim, "No time," I drove and waited for him in the car.

Returning, he reported, "He says I have diverticulitis."

Although he didn't give it voice, Bob seemed unconvinced.

Another month went by. He shed more weight. I tried a new approach, appealing to his long-held desire to take care of me. "I know you don't think you need further tests and you're probably right, but I need you to have them for my peace of mind."

Agreed. In November, I accompanied him to a radiologist's office where he would have a CAT scan. In the waiting room he complained about having to drink copious amounts of viscous, chalky liquid. "I can't do any more of this," he said with anger. Experience with this not infrequently irascible husband had taught me that such a pronouncement could foretell an abrupt, annoyed departure and so I asked the nurse if he could forgo the last dose. Because she'd been gentle and attentive, I wasn't surprised when she smiled and said, "Of course."

The next day, I took her flowers in appreciation for her kindness throughout the procedure. She said, "I think he'll be fine." But, there was something in her eye, a brief flicker. She'd seen something on the scan. I replied, "He has to be, he's a lovely man." I wept for the first time in a long time. At an early age, we Lazears had been trained out of tears. "Lazears don't cry." "Be a stoic." "Be plucky." And we didn't and we were.

"You'll have the results after the weekend."

The Answer

AND WE DID.

Bob called from his office, "Looks like pancreatic cancer." Just like that. Matter of fact.

So, this was how our love affair was to end. Of course. It was too passionate, too fervid to fizzle from waning interest, fading sexual ardor or devotion. It would never have died of its own accord. With sudden, searing certainty I determined to love this man out of life as love had brought our child into it.

I knew with this pronouncement that he was going to die, was dying, would soon be dead. Two of our friends had gone before him. I knew he would die in approximately three months. Pancreatic cancer is straightforward that way. By the time you catch it it's too late. By the time you catch your breath, it might be your last. By the time you've felt sick long enough to go to a doctor and when that doctor delivers the diagnosis, you'd better have made plans. This disease would move as quickly and intensely as our falling in love. The ending as fast as the beginning.

I knew all this but matched my tone to his. I was tearless, "plucky," and matter of fact, as though discussing the quotidian matters of domestic life. What to have for dinner, when to buy next year's calendar. We were in sync. We knew that if one of us were to weep, it would cause the other inordinate pain. From the start of our relationship, we were bound by the desire to uplift one another. So, now, on the phone we were brave for one another.

One could argue that this quality was a result of our awareness that it was likely he would predecease me. When we'd married, I at

21 and he at 42, I'd accepted those odds. If this were the Preakness, you wouldn't bet on that old horse. I did.

But I thought that with enough practice I would be a match for whatever befell us. To that end when I was on writing assignments far afield, I ate alone in restaurants, good restaurants frequented by couples. I ordered wine — fine wine to accompany a fine meal. No book to keep me from looking at other diners looking at me. Alone. No thank you, to the table behind the potted palm and no cowardly room service... ever. I entered those places with a rehearsed air of confidence, determined to get the hang of it. Granted, the first few times I wanted to put a sign on the table declaring, "I could get a date if I wanted one."

For his part, Bob would point out various office file drawers. "This is where..." I'd find whatever I would need in the event of his death. In the event of... Here were patients' records, "Burn them," to protect their anonymity and the sacred privacy of the consulting room. A sacred burning. Here was the life insurance policy. Here two honorable discharges from naval service in WW II and Korea. "The V.A. helps with funeral expenses." Here was his poetry, "In case you want to keep it." Here a folder of our love letters. Here was a folder with mementos and letters from his first marriage to Carol. "Please give these to her."

Bank statements. Deeds. Receipts.

He would lose me somewhere between burning files and Vets and funerals.

From the start of our (illicit, scandalous) unlikely love affair, we'd faced and prepared for this eventuality.

I understood our finances, did half the accounting, had overseen a lengthy, at times bullying, IRS audit single handed, had power of attorney and credit cards in my name. I could change a tire, check the oil, snake a toilet. I remembered to keep fresh batteries in the flashlights, steer by the white line to the right of the road when driving through fog or into bright headlights. I could roast a chicken that would last four days. I reasoned I had what it took to manage on my own.

Yes, I had what it took. No matter that in the early days of our marriage I put my hands over my ears when Bob would say, "When I die, the greatest testament to our love would be for you to fall in love and marry again."

No, no, no. You. Only you. Forever.

He would smile and say, "Love begets more love."

But no, our calm wasn't the result of years of preparation.

"What do we do now?"

"Go see David this afternoon after my last patient."

Of course, he'd see his scheduled patients. He was a psychiatrist who wouldn't leave them feeling abandoned. Until they were. He looked after them as a beneficent guardian. I'd once asked, "How do you stand it if a patient is a pain in the ass?"

"I treat their humanity," said he.

I thought of Eudora Welty who once told me in an interview, "I love all my characters. The good ones and the villains."

The Buddha taught that all people possess Buddha nature, the capacity for generosity, compassion, loving kindness, patience. I was hard pressed to find that in the merely annoying. But, I believe that is what Bob was attempting to help his patients uncover. His compassion went in search of theirs. He honored the optimism and courage that brought the broken to his doorstep.

When he became too ill to continue seeing them in his office, after consulting with me, he offered to see them at home thus upending the strictly adhered to sacred anonymity of the consultation room. Because it was not in his nature to pull punches, he'd informed them that he was dying. Some wanted to hold on until the end. Just one more insight. Just one more moment of wisdom. I bought him a navy blue, paisley, silk dressing gown for these sessions. Opening our apartment door, I met the formerly anonymous face to face. I would only learn their names later from sympathy letters. "Without Dr. Ascher, I wouldn't be here today…" wrote someone he'd talked back from the edge. He had never had a suicide. It was as though he had a Blood Hound's nose for a mind. If he sensed that possibility, off to the hospital until the danger passed. Like that.

The middle-aged, the old and those who appeared to be on the cusp of thirty crossed our threshold. When he reached sixty-five, he'd stopped accepting adolescent patients, an age group for which he had an affinity, "Because they deserve someone who can hang in until they grow up." Grow up. Once he came home later than usual because a patient dressing for a prom asked to return at the end of the day so Bob could tie his bow tie. He did and Bob did.

Naturally, patients' appreciation wasn't unanimous. Whenever Bob appeared haggard over dinner, I knew that there'd been a whole lot of shoutin' goin' on.

I also knew when he was seeing patients gratis. Simple. Money would run short. Civil rights workers, priests, ministers, nuns, the young who sought treatment but whose parents wouldn't pay, other physicians and their families. He believed that the Hippocratic oath required one to treat doctors and their children and spouses as family. And because he was a "Doctor's, doctor" there were many for whom there was no charge.

One of these, a colleague whom Bob had suggested his patients consult "following my death," told me that when he visited him in the hospital to learn about the referrals, "The hour was like a great grand rounds. I wish every resident could have been there to hear his presentation. I've never heard anything like it. That degree of insight, eloquence and compassion. When he was finished, I knew that person and knew what he needed. Without meeting them, I already cared."

I admired those who came through our door, the stouthearted willing to witness their doctor's frailty. I praised Bob for being open to it. Was it therapy or a long goodbye? A bit of both.

These visits would not have occurred had Bob not forgone the earlier, classic, Freudian, cool remove in which he'd been sternly trained by Viennese analysts trained in turn by Freud. After years of practice, he'd concluded, "It's ridiculous that everything is considered transference, including 'good morning and goodbye.'"

Yes. Ridiculous. Once, following a session, my own analyst registered surprise verging on panic, an "Oh, no!" expression when upon leaving the office he saw that I was still in the hall waiting for a slow elevator. He headed to the back stairs scampering down all eight flights rather than share the ride with me.

Long ago Bob had given his patients our home phone number in case of emergency. They never called. He learned that it was unnecessary to be cold and remote in order to retain his equanimity and objectivity. When appropriate, he mourned and rejoiced with them, encouraged and cheered them on, shared his faith in them.

As planned, that afternoon we went to David, who had received a copy of the diagnosis and agreed to see us as soon as we could get there. His nurse ushered us out of the waiting room before the front door had swung shut. "Oh, Dr. Ascher. Dr. Ascher. It's always so wonderful to see you."

She showed us to the consulting room where David sat behind a wide, deep, wooden desk, his shield from pain and contagion. It held totems. Photographs of wife, children, grandchildren. Life, life, life.

Bob and he began to speak with clinical remove, professional to professional as though discussing a shared patient. This husband of mine was as steady as he'd been on the phone and when we'd greeted each other at home with a silent embrace. This man of passion and easy tears, sudden tempers and deep tenderness was able to be clinical rather than emotional, "Who do you recommend as an oncologist?"

"I think you should see our man at New York Hospital," he said referring to the favored oncologist at the hospital with which Bob and David were affiliated. Because, he explained, "They tend to get lost between the cracks at Memorial," the go to cancer center.

"They." Already the separation. Already the nameless. Not patient. Not the dying. "They." I would soon become familiar with this remove, with physicians' assiduous avoidance of the word, "death." To do otherwise would be to admit defeat and no matter the odds, they were in the business of defying death. They weren't going to discuss the possibility of losing a round.

"Fine then." It was decided. An appointment was made.

We assumed the attitude of voyagers following a strict itinerary in Rome. 9 a.m. cappuccino. Read what Hugh Honour has to say about the Pantheon. 10 a.m. visit the Pantheon. Pay homage at Virgil's tomb. Don't neglect to look up at the open ceiling. The round open ceiling. Wonder at the ageless hunger for light. Wonder at the comfort of a circle. Read Jung on the circle.

As long as we stuck to the itinerary, its dictates would distract from the destination.

When David sent Bob down the hall to have bloods drawn, I remained behind. The first of unspoken agreements. I would stay behind to hear what wasn't said. I would stay behind and be brave. I would be the testing tree. Throw rocks at me and I'd stay firmly rooted. I was confident that I was good at this.

With his back to me as he washed his hands he said, "The news couldn't be worse,"

"I know."

When I met Bob back in the waiting room, I helped him into his coat. He had grown thin and needed protection against October's early chill.

He didn't need the help, but we'd been doing this for a long time. For over thirty-four years, I'd held his coat, patted him on the back and called after him as he went out the door to work, "You're off to be the wizard."

He helped me into mine and as always, I had to ask him to bend down so the sleeves weren't above my head beyond my reach. He was a foot taller than I. We had our patterns.

Back home we called our thirty-three-year-old daughter, Rebecca and my now middle-aged stepchildren Elizabeth (Lizzie), Ellen and Steven (Steve.) I emailed their mother, Bob's former wife, Carol, a thoughtful and caring member of what Steve's wife Jeannie called, "this one, big, crazy family." With the exception of Ellen in California, they all lived near one another in Cambridge.

"Your dad has pancreatic cancer," I told them. I didn't say, prepare for a world without him. Bob the patriarch was a force of nature for good and bad, how could they imagine such a world let alone prepare for it? Steve a documentary filmmaker and the youngest at 46 years old, would one day make a short film, a fictional son's conflicts with a fictional father who was (spoiler alert!) a psychiatrist. Said son "wished" his father dead, "But I didn't want him to die."

Siblings born to the same parents enter different families. Steve's misfortune was to arrive at a time of escalating animosity between his parents. He was caught in the crossfire of an unhappy marriage and Bob's long, analytic training and analysis that kept him in the city late at night after a long day's practice. When he was at home, he was tense, exhausted and angry. Unlike Rebecca's and my experience with him as husband and father, in those early days, newly steeped in Freud, and perhaps with the zeal of a recent convert, he had failed to have learned one of the most important edicts: confine the practice to the consulting room. Thus, where his young son was concerned there was "diagnosis" in place of compassion. Rather than being sympathetic to the nine-year-old's bedwetting, he considered it ominous. He blamed the mother. He blamed some Freudian deviance. The truth was that some children, mostly boys, continue to wet their beds into late childhood, grow out of it and don't become criminals or hobbled human beings.

Perhaps most sad is that there is a genetic c
sis which made it all the more pitiful that Bob
bed wetter failed to put his arm around Stev
let him know he'd been there, it would pass.

But we can be blindsided in the raising
inciting rather than informing. None of
errors on that battleground rife with demons. Our children a
often the victims of "friendly fire." Freud said, there are two things
impossible to do right, raise children and govern nations. Wrongs
recollected haunt a parent at 4 a.m. Had Steve's film been made
and Bob seen it before his death, I know he would have acknowledged and been horrified by his wrongheaded cruelty. He would
have apologized to the son he adored and to whom he had caused
harm. He would have said as he did to me one day when he was
older, wiser, safer, and I pointed out how he had hurt my feelings,
"What a terrible way to treat someone you love." He could see it,
accept it, be remorseful and sympathetic. But back then it had been
a terrible way to treat a son he loved.

So much changes when one is secure in love. No longer are
fear's offspring — anger and aggression clouding the mind. Those
emotions don't disappear, but erupt less frequently. One day on the
tennis court we watched a father berate his young son who weeping said, "But I'm just a little boy." Bob's response to me was, "The
worst thing you can do is to shame a child." I'm not sure whether
he was thinking of his own little boy. And what a pity that wisdom
comes so late and slow. For all of us.

The Bob I knew came through the door after work joyful to be
home having left Freud tied to a chair, masking tape on his mouth,
locked in the office. Sometimes the teenaged Rebecca and I found
this annoying when we wanted to share a dream we'd found fascinating. "Nope. Workday's done." He was true to that for as long
as we knew him. He was the father who bathed baby Rebecca, read

bedtime story and when she was old enough to sit up, put her
his shoulders and signaled her to duck, "Low bridge" before
going through her bedroom's doorway.

When she "popped," or rather, was yanked out with high for-
ceps following a difficult labor Bob looked at her and said, "Here
is our love child." He never stopped feeling that way nor did she
question his adoration. It would have been natural for the older
three to resent this addition to the family who was not only well
loved; she got to live with us full time. Instead they claimed their
baby sister and carried her around as an appendage, showing her
off to their friends and even their mother who was gracious and
extended invitations to her as she grew. Such generosity of spirit
resulted in the four considering themselves sisters and brother. In
all these years, they have never spoken of each other as half siblings. As adults, Lizzie and Rebecca are best friends.

Rebecca, mystified by Steve's portrayal of Bob, told him, "This
is a father I never knew. But then, I had a different mother." A
different mother because I had not suffered Carol's experience.
A different mother because I didn't have three young children in
addition to an admittedly "complex" husband who could have a
temper tantrum because she'd forgotten to buy milk. A different
mother in that I was cherished. A different mother in that I fanned
her little girl enthusiasm for him. By example, I demonstrated,
"This is the man we love." I didn't have to shield myself, I didn't
have to struggle to earn and hold his love.

Carol was beautiful and had so much charm that all ages fell in
love with her. Therefore, it was a mystery why that had not happened with Bob. No one can understand another's marriage. It is
only with difficulty that we understand our own. What I do know
is that neither party is to "blame" when a marriage fails, and that
happenstance and personal histories are among the culprits behind
a mismatched pair.

Hearing of the diagnosis, Lizzie the physician buried herself in research that in her gloom she would present as dramatically dire. Ellen, the middle child offered to fly in from California. Steve was quiet, as is his wont. And Rebecca, who'd grown up expecting her older father, forty-four when she was born would die when she still needed him, accepted the news as inevitable. We each responded and began to cope in different ways. Throughout the ordeal, we'd give each other room to do so.

Bob and I wanted no room. That night after dinner he washed the dishes as he always had, "You cook it, I clean up." We went to bed and didn't break our embrace until the morning alarm.

Oncologist

THE NEXT AFTERNOON, when we arrived at the designated address, Rebecca and I caught each other's eyes. Our communications had always been strong whether silent or articulated. Were we at the right place? I double-checked the slip of paper in my pocket. Yes, and we didn't have a good feeling about this homely building squatting on a dark side street in the shadows of taller structures. Could we trust a doctor whose locus of practice lacked any redeeming, aesthetic value?

We'd imagined something more in line with other doctors' offices on the ground floor of gracious, pre-war, residential, apartment buildings on sunlit avenues. We became suspicious. We'd already begun to read the world for auspices and omens. We'd already begun to assume an aspect of primitive thinking that emerges in the face of disaster.

We took the elevator to the fourth floor. It was getting worse. The door opened onto a waiting room of patients whose appearance varied in proportion to their despair. Some sat with private duty nurses, alone or with family members attempting cheerful chatter if they had any left. Some shuffled to the magazine rack dragging their I.V. tubes behind them.

I didn't wonder if they'd live. I didn't wonder if they were beating the odds. I had only one concern — the care of my husband. My focus was as intense and singular as a welder with a torch.

The windows were dirty and the walls bore the beige tone that results when painters are instructed, "Whatever doesn't show the dirt." I'd seen the cheap furniture in one of Bob's office supply catalogues. There were no flowers, no art, no privacy. Nothing to divert the mind from thoughts of doom as poisonous chemicals dripped into veins. I recognized a man who lived in our building. We averted our eyes.

Gray faces in gray chairs in gray air.

A sullen woman sitting behind smudged glass took offense as Bob announced himself, "I'm here to see…"

"I'll get to you. Go sit down."

A seed of fury was planted in me. It would grow over the next months until it became the fuel that propelled my forceful insistence on Bob's being afforded the respect he deserved and the care he required. But for now, I stayed seated. The disease against which we would rage had made us meek. We needed these people. We didn't have to like them, but we needed them.

I whispered to Rebecca, "This looks like an abortion clinic pre Roe v. Wade." She nodded and rolled her eyes.

We sat and sat. Twenty, thirty, thirty-five minutes past our appointed time, Bob was ready to leave. He had that restless look I knew as well as I knew coming changes of weather when we sailed off the New England coast. I knew when it was time to tie a reef in his emotional sails. "I'm not waiting any longer. Let's get out of here." So predictable. Patience was not his strong suit.

"Sweetheart, we've waited this long. It will take even more of your time if you have to make another appointment and get back down here."

Saved. A short, white haired man with a slow gait and a paunch that strained against the buttons of his white coat entered the room and called our name. Well-worn smile lines rendered his face gentle. "I apologize. I don't usually keep patients waiting." His demeanor was so gracious that our apprehension softened. We followed him down the hall to his office and sat facing a standard issue desk. Rebecca struggled to steady herself on the only remaining chair — unbalanced and absent an arm. She and I looked at each other and directed our gazes to a framed New York Magazine cover, "Best Doctors in New York." Reassuring. We studied the family photos on the wall. Posed. Self-consciously proper. The young girls and women crossed their ankles just so. One woman was caught in mid-delight. His wife?

He sat down across from us behind a clutter of what I hoped were gifts from grateful patients. A monogramed letter opener, a book about wine, a silver tray engraved with the name of the hospital and date of the gift.

I liked his full lips those smile lines. His hair matched his coat and I wondered why he cut it in a Napoleonic style. The places a mind goes.

The questions began. The call and response. How much exercise? Appetite? The getting-to-know-you-chat carried on as though death weren't snickering in the corner.

"I play tennis twice a week," Bob said with pride. He wanted to be seen as more than his disease. A father and a tennis player. He spoke of the three doctors in the family, Elizabeth, her husband Michael and Rebecca's husband Chuck.

"So, where's the rest of the family?"

"Chuck's in surgery and Steve and Lizzie live in Cambridge. Ellen's in San Diego. Elizabeth's a cardiologist, Steve's a documentary film maker…" I reached for Bob's hand, I could tell he was about to say that a film made by him and his wife had been nominated for an Academy Award after winning the Grand Jury Prize and Audience Award at Sundance Film Festival. He turned to me and smiled. "I know. I'm talking too much."

"No you aren't." Yes, he was. He was talking too much and I wanted to get down to the facts.

I noticed a basket of apples on the floor. O.K. this guy couldn't be all bad. He'd gone apple picking over the weekend.

Bob asked the big question, "What's the next step?"

Dr. P suggested chemo. "Gemzar works pretty well in these

cases." What did that mean? What did "work" mean? What did "well" mean? We all knew that this was a disease that thumbed its nose at any substance sent to vanquish it. Rebecca and I knew how Bob would respond.

For years he'd been telling us, "Put a bullet through my head," under such circumstances. Put a bullet through his head if he could no longer sail, play tennis, make wild and crazy love. Put a bullet through his head if he was diagnosed with an incurable disease.

But he didn't say, "No chemo." He quickly and firmly said, "Let's do it."

Let's do it?

His determined response signaled Rebecca and me that we were not to say, "Hey! You always said…" That was the beginning of understanding that we'd entered territory where "always" was a nonsense word. The punch line to a joke.

As a physician Bob knew chemotherapy's possible ravages. He knew how it could take a body to the brink of death and if the patient survived and the cancer did not, well, you might just have a chance. But, he had no chances.

"Are you always this thin?" A note was scrawled on a piece of paper to be inserted into a chart that would grow and grow and grow. "We're a skinny family," I said glancing at Bob's long, lean frame that looked great in clothes. Any clothes. I'd fallen in love with that body the way we fall in love with certain aspects of a person long before we know them or know we're in love.

"I want you to put on ten pounds before we start treatment."

And that was that. It was good to have an assignment, homework, an agenda. A project. Fattening up. As we went for our coats I announced with cheer, "We'll go to the soda fountain on 83rd and Lex. for milkshakes." Oh, good idea! Everyone agreed! A reward! Ice cream for the good children! We demonstrated delight short of clapping our hands. Oh, goody, goody. Chocolate syrup. Yum.

This was Barbara in Crisis. A cool calm takes over moving like a glacier across my mental landscape. I make lists. I make plans. When I was in my fiery twenties and had a tendency to ride the outsized emotional responses not uncommon to that age, Bob trying to lend me a hand out of confusion would ask, "Can't you take a step of distance from your emotions?" Are you kidding? In your twenties, you are your emotions. Why should I take a step of distance from what affirmed a passionate life force? In spite of the misery they cause, in ones twenties there is also something perversely delicious about the unchecked rush of hate, fear, jealously, love. Proof you're really alive. Yes, I was mature enough to be a wife, mother, stepmother but it takes the twenties to wipe away the last strands of adolescent detritus.

Now in crisis, as when twelve years ago I'd learned that Bobby, my younger brother by twelve years had AIDS which at that time was devoid of hope or help, and nine years after that, learned of my father's inoperable Glioblastoma, I took more than that step of distance Bob thought essential for understanding and clarity. I left emotion on the opposite end of a football field. I determined to be the calm caregiver, to be strong. We all know the eventual price for that, but for now so be it.

"I'll be right back," I said and walked back in the direction from which we'd come. I wanted to ask one more question. The doctor was in the hall on his way to the next patient. He paused at my approach. "How long have we got?" I asked.

Bob hadn't asked the same question because he didn't have to. A keen clinician and diagnostician, he'd had the training and experience to know the answer. I, on the other hand when confronted with chaos, want facts, specifics. Landmarks for the lost.

"Nobody can tell you that." Again that smile.

"O.K., then," I pushed my point, "Should I buy a Thanksgiving turkey?" He laughed. No, he giggled, something we'd learn he did often enough for us to begin referring to him as "the giggling oncologist." "Yes. Buy a Thanksgiving turkey."

Good. So we had three weeks. Sometimes you have to trick them into telling you what they know.

I added, "And I want you to be truthful with me at all times. I can deal with the truth. I can't deal with evasions and politesse. Don't 'spare' me. I want you to be absolutely straight and keep me up to date." The latter was important, I knew from both my father's and brother's fatal illnesses. It becomes the new reality of the moment. It was agreed.

I rejoined Bob and Rebecca and in silence we drove to the last, remaining soda fountain in our neighborhood, one that still served soft drinks in 1950's style glasses with "Coca Cola" scrolled on them. It had been staying the course since 1925 when Bob was one-year-old. It was hard to imagine that much had changed. The "linen" Formica counter worn through where plates had been passed and elbows propped across the years. The speckled yellow, brown and beige linoleum floor with its nod to Art Deco in the design around the stools. The place smelled like a griddle with a history. Burgers, bacon, eggs, home fries spatula flipped again and again and again. I never left without that history's scent in my hair.

Once seated in front of the Danish pastry that looked like every other Danish pastry served in diners and coffee shops across the country, Rebecca began swinging her leg as she always did to relieve tension. I stared at the black and white photos on the wall. Reba, the owner with Woody Allen, Bruce Springsteen, Uma Thurman, Bill Clinton. He'd been behind this counter for as long as I'd been coming here. He didn't look up from the griddle on which he pressed a grilled cheese sandwich flat, sending the scent of burnt butter and cheddar into the air. With a practiced hand he lifted and slapped the sandwich onto a white plate he put in front of the man who sat at the other end of the counter. Turning to us, all business, no smile, he awaited our orders.

God help you if you hadn't made up your mind. Chocolate, coffee no syrup, vanilla. The practiced swing and reach into deep, cardboard containers, the flick of the wrist and click of the latch to release the ice cream from the scoop. I watched him squirt the syrup, pour the milk — whole milk — good. My mind was eased by the regular motions of his work life. Basic. A beginning, middle and at the end something delicious. Something contained within its routine.

When the shakes were poured — a slow, thick, ice-cream-lumpy pour, when they were placed in front of us and we'd pushed our straws through the satisfactory thickness, only then did we begin to speak.

"So, what do you think?" Bob asked.

"About which aspect?"

"The oncologist."

Rebecca shrugged. I shrugged.

Silence as we sucked on our straws. Slurp, slurp at the end. Rebecca hated that when I went for the last, noisy sip.

"Thank you," to the owner and down from our stools while Bob paid and tipped.

Back home, later in the day I heard him on the phone with our financial advisor, Sheila Horwitz. Without self-pity and sounding more like a meteorologist, "wind from the northeast," he told her, "I have pancreatic cancer and I need you to promise that you'll take care of Barbie." He paused, "I mean, take care of her as though she were your own daughter." Our savings and retirement accounts were so minimal, they could be overlooked, not worth bothering with or worried over. There was a pause at his end of the phone followed by a corrective, "I know exactly where I am going." When I asked about this, he told me that Sheila with whom he'd shared twenty years of affection and advice had responded to the news with, "You're not going anywhere."

Who knows where the dead "go," if they do "go." What Bob did know was that he was leaving us. He wanted safeguards in place.

I went into my office and once again emailed the other three children. It was important to bring them up to date at the same time, so nobody was more in the loop than the rest. Where death is involved such moments can splinter families and I wanted to be very, very careful. We needed and would continue to need each other now, at the end, and after.

I told them about the trip to the soda fountain and my determination to have one celebration a day. One special treat. A toast to life. A reminder of its sweetness, its delights. I urged them to do the same. "I don't care if it's a finer wine than we usually drink or a chocolate truffle, or ice cream anytime we want it. We mustn't forget to celebrate."

Steve called to report that he'd researched Gemzar on line. It was relatively new but getting good reports for its efficacy and minimum side effects.

That night, Bob and I dined by candlelight. I suggested that over the next week we think about whether there was anything we would like to tell one another? Had there been anything left unsaid? Any grudges, any left over negative emotions, any withheld apologies, any unexpressed gratitude or love? I wanted us to speak the unspoken before it was too late.

He agreed and taking my hand said, "I've had a good life. But this is a terrible abandonment of you."

"No," I protested. "You've made my life so happy. Being forced to leave me is not willful abandonment." Little did I know that abandoned was precisely how I would feel when this chapter ended.

Staring at a framed photo he'd taken of the Grand Canal and hung on the wall across from the dining table so we could dream on it, he said, "I would have liked to go to Venice again." No whining. There won't be any whining. There was a long pause and then a smile, "But that's just me being greedy."

"Who can blame you?" I reminded him, "You said on our last visit, 'Venice makes it okay to die.'"

Upon arrival in and until our departure from that city, Bob

heard music. He would ask me repeatedly, "Do you hear it?" No, I could not. One night he awakened me. His cheeks were covered with tears, "Now do you hear it?" I took him into my arms. "I'm sorry, I don't."

"It's so beautiful," said he.

I wondered if it was T.S. Eliot's "music heard so deeply/That it is not heard at all, but you are the music/While the music lasts." Or the sounds Bach heard before transforming them to notes on paper. Or Wordsworth's "notes that are/The ghostly language of the ancient earth…" Who knows? For me, it was one of those mysteries that didn't require an answer. What mattered was that it had made Bob think that it was o.k. to die.

The following week, we sat down for dinner and as we always had, raised our glasses to one another, held hands and had a moment of silence before eating. "So, anything?" I asked, referring to the suggestion that we articulate all we would want the other to know. He was quiet and shook his head, no. "You?"

"No."

What we both knew was that with the exception of when we were pissed off at each other, we had never failed to express our love. When I was at home rather than on a travel assignment for the New York Times or some other magazine, we did so three meals a day. Every night before sleep. Sometimes in the quietude that follows a fight.

Months ago, before we knew anything, when our lives were moving along as usual, when we were in the car running errands of a Saturday — picking up dry cleaning, buying wine, taking shoes to the cobbler — when we came to a stoplight, Bob reached for my hand and continuing to look straight ahead said, "You are my heartbeat."

No. No unexpressed love.

"It Was the Love that Swallows Up All Else"
— William Carlos Williams

IT WAS A LOVE AGAINST ALL ODDS. It was courageous and bold and like grief, insisted upon itself. Love is not blind, it is discerning. It is a challenging discernment that demands we follow its course, and we do because there is no course.

Bob, looking back over the years would say, "I don't know how I had the courage. I'm not a brave man." Nor was he a temperate man. His waiting to proclaim his love had been out of character. His passions tended to rule for better or worse. But, in this he had kept his own counsel.

"And I never had the courage for naughtiness. I was such a good girl." I certainly would never have condoned an extramarital affair. How did I have the fortitude to defy my parents who were as horrified by that defiance as they were by the news that I was going to marry outside the tribe. He was a Jew from New York. An about to be divorced Jew from New York. Better than a still married Jew from New York, I thought. "We've never known a divorced person." He was older than I, "He'll die." "He's a psychiatrist. Maybe he hypnotized her. This isn't Barbie." How did I take on three adolescent children as though that were natural rather than a challenge? Nothing about our individual responses was in keeping with who we had been. We were no longer who we had been.

Love cracks us open to the truth of who we are, a revelation with the caveat that we respond to what is revealed. It exhorts as Thomas does in the Gnostic Gospels, "If you bring forth what is within you, what you bring forth will save you. If you do not bring forth what is within you, what you do not bring forth will destroy you." We knew this to be true.

Lovers are wont to credit the hand of fate, but what is fate other than an attempt to explain the inexplicable? Love and death are two great mysteries thumbing their noses at our explanations.

We're familiar with conversion stories of the saints and saintly, their "seeing," "hearing," "feeling" the spirit upon them. What we are not told is why. To ask that is to ask the wrong question. By happenstance they were standing at the intersection of time and timelessness. That's all. And that's everything.

What is told is that they "knew." They experienced a new kind of "knowing," love that inspired them to drop their nets, profligacy, wealth, the outside world and to follow the call no matter the costs. As with earthly love, the costs were dear.

We know of their professed, "dark nights of the soul," "thunderous seas," "barren winters" when faith was lost and they forgot its reason for being. So it is with profound love between ordinary mortals. It is constant through those dark nights that obscure it. It is steadfast as we throw the plate, stamp the foot, slam the door, say we're leaving. To live love is not to experience one long, steady miracle, although that's what it is. When we are blinded by the confusions of being human it's there waiting for our vision to clear.

I visualized Bob's and my love as a living thing, an amorphous orb that hovered between us. It required care and nurturing. Whenever I lost my way, it never lost its way. I knew that it was bigger than each of us, that it held firm when we flailed about in folly. We would not abandon it any more than we would abandon a child. It depended on us.

The moment of Bob's seeing and knowing was not wished for there and then, not that late summer evening when we met. Another time, perhaps. He was unprepared for that abrupt, terrible awareness. Like grace, such a moment is unbidden but there it is and you'd better pay attention. Don't expect it to happen again.

Hospital

TWO WEEKS AFTER DIAGNOSIS, two hours after dinner and reading poetry to one another as had been our habit, one hour after he'd showered, powdered himself and dressed in pressed, blue, cotton pajamas, I tucked Bob into bed and leaned over, pressing into his soapy scent, the long firm sinew of his body. He was an elegant man abed or on rising.

And then, we had our first crisis. He groaned. I had never heard this sound. He strained across the bed for the phone and called David. "Take sodium phosphate." I threw on my jacket, leashed the dog and raced five blocks to the nearest, open drugstore.

Back home, Gabriel, our black standard poodle flopped onto the floor close to Bob's side of the bed. Bob swallowed the laxative and we waited for stomach rumbles, the miracle of a body responding to directives. Nothing. "Shall I give you another dose?" I did and again nothing. His belly was round and hard, his moans more frequent. He called David again. An enema.

The cancer had locked him in its mad dog jaws
Back into the night to the pharmacy. Back home. No results.
"I think maybe we'd better get you to the hospital."
"No."

I anticipated this response. To go to the hospital would be to surrender control, something physicians are loathe to do. He only agreed once he took charge by making a diagnosis, diminishing the sovereignty of pain by naming it. "I'm obstructed."

No, no ambulance, he insisted. That would be for a seriously sick person. Who could blame him for clinging to his past, healthy self? He was a man of accomplishment and formidable intelligence, a violinist, respected physician, a tennis player with a cannon ball serve, a sailor who could catch the last whiff of wind and ride it home while others were becalmed. This man who knew how to work with the vagaries of time and tide was not going to be carried out on a stretcher and strapped into the back of an ambulance.

He would drive himself. And no, he wouldn't wait in the lobby while I got the car. He managed to smile at the doorman and walk with me to the garage. Once behind the wheel he was no longer helpless. Taking charge distracted from the pain.

He parked in his usual spot in the doctors' garage, a privilege that gave him pleasure, as did his white coat and badge. Yes, he was a real doctor. We walked into the emergency room where I suggested he sit while I told the woman behind the desk, "My husband is seriously ill and in agonizing pain. Please have someone see him quickly."

"Everybody here is seriously ill." Of course, she was right, but in crisis' narrowing of focus I couldn't register that.

"Not like this," I wanted to say. I'd never witnessed pain like this but then, I'd never been on a battlefield.

I wasn't going to wait. I walked through the doors to the nearest nurse. "My husband has to be seen immediately."

In we went, onto a bed around which a curtain was snapped like a sheet before being hung on a clothesline. Off with the loafers, the tweed sports jacket, blue and white striped shirt, flannel trousers and plaid boxers. "Leave your socks on. Your feet will get cold," I suggested as I tied the back of the standard issue hospital gown. Those gowns are the first step in dehumanizing a patient. Individuals can be dangerous. They could cause you to care. "Patients should be able to choose their gowns," I muttered. There are so many ways to make hospitals more humane. To remind the "caregivers" (hated expression) that they care for humans.

A resident appeared and probed Bob's belly, retreated and returned to say, "We have to take you to surgery." Meanwhile, Demerol was administered. Merciful Demerol. Except it wasn't making any difference. I gave it ten minutes before going in search of help.

"Please, give my husband more pain medication."

"I can't"

"Yes you can."

"I've given him the limit."

"But it's not doing anything."

We were squaring off. A frightened resident and an equally frightened wife. Fear made us each stand our ground. His protocol. My husband.

Time passed and pain increased; I repeated my plea to no avail. "What? You're afraid he might become addicted?" He didn't note the irony.

We'd arrived at 8:30 and by 1 a.m. there were still no beds upstairs and no surgeon. The pain's growing intensity sent me back to the nurses' station. "Why is it taking so long?"

"Emergencies. Back up."

"This is an emergency."

"The doctor was in surgery when you arrived and it turned out to be complicated."

I was tempted to wheel Bob up to the O.R., through the doors into the cold scent of anesthesia and the sharp clang of tools, park him next to the anesthetized patient and say to the surgeon, "You've got two hands don't you?"

Barring that, I asked for morphine and something was administered, again to little avail. Bob began to shake and I went to raid empty cubicles of blankets. I made a note to bring our own and a hot water bottle the next time. Lots of hot water bottles.

I wrapped him in the blankets and leaned down to embrace him careful to avoid his stomach, willing my arms and torso to exude heat. Sometimes it worked. When Rebecca was a child and suffering from fever and chills, I'd climb into bed, hold her close to my body and think, "heat." I would in fact become warm enough to stop her chills. That magic was not working here. We didn't need magic we needed the surgeon. And with that, he walked in. See, magic. He was young, handsome, smiling and explained his delay. "A complication."

After examining Bob, he announced that he would have to perform a colonoscopy to relieve the blockage. Of course, there was the possibility that he might have to perform an ileostomy. He hoped not. "They can be messy. The bags tend to burst."

Untenable for fastidious Bob, I thought. This was a man who shined his shoes before wearing them, a man who tied his bow ties with attentive care, who shaved twice a day if he thought his stubble would irritate my skin, who came to bed each night scrubbed clean. No, no ileostomy for shaving brush, shoeshine brush Bob.

A colostomy, he continued, was pretty straightforward. Open a cavity in the side of his torso and attach a bag to catch the body's waste. An anus where one of his saddle soaped belts should be.

"Sometimes once the patient heals, the incision can be closed and normal bowel movements resume."

Not so in the case of an ileostomy. In that event a nurse would teach me how to empty the pouches.

Why did he bother explaining all this? Under stress and sleeplessness, I couldn't make sense of it. All I wanted was for Bob to be relieved.

By 3 a.m., Rebecca who had arrived after I'd called her and I were ushered into his assigned room. An hour later, Chuck who had finished his last surgical case, and my stepson's wife, Jeannie, who upon hearing the news of the surgery had gotten on a bus from Cambridge, joined us.

Little was said. What was there to say? And we were tired. So very, very tired. We leaned forward in our chairs and put our heads on the bed, hoping for sleep that didn't come.

Four hours later, the surgeon walked through the door. He'd had to perform an ileostomy.

Exhaustion muffled everything. What was he saying? All I wanted was my bed.

Chuck stayed behind as the rest of us readied to leave. "Somebody has to be in the recovery room to tell him what's happened when he wakes up." Of course Chuck would think of that. His kindness was natural, unstudied. Yes, he was the right choice. The two of them shared an intense and loving bond. More father and son than in-laws.

When we'd met him soon after Rebecca had on her first day as a college freshman, Bob had said to me, "Let's try not to fall in love with him. In case it doesn't last." But there was no avoiding falling in love with him, his wry humor, easygoing manner, generosity and intelligence. His love for and care of our daughter. Chuck in turn, adopted us and was soon spending summers under our roof. He had a difficult relationship with his own father and was eager for a surrogate. He followed in Bob's footsteps, attended his medical school and upon graduation, Bob gave him his diploma. Yes. Chuck, a surgeon himself would deliver the news with his characteristic compassion and reassuring manner.

The next morning, when I came to Bob's bedside, he smiled and reached for my hand. I took hold and kissed his forehead, allowing my lips to linger there.

"How are you?" Silly question.

"I'm sorry. This is going to be hard for you. I think I should stay here for quite a while."

"No. I'll miss you too much."

"But you'd have to take care of…"

"I know and it's fine. I'll watch and learn how. I want you at home. I want you by my side."

I asked if he were in a lot of pain?

"No." He pointed to the i.v. morphine and added, "I'm more

worried about you."

"You're the one who's just had brutal surgery, not I. Don't worry about me."

Don't worry. Such a ridiculous phrase, a powerless verbal tic.

When the nurse arrived to clean his wound, I pretended to watch and listen to her instructions but could not. I strived for an attentive demeanor devoid of emotion but gazed at the side of the bed rather than Bob's torso. Once she left he repeated, "I'm so sorry."

I put my arms around his shoulders, pressing my head against his heart. Thump, thump, thump. Iambic pentameter — the rhythm of life.

"I love you. I love you. I love you. You have nothing to be sorry for."

I stood up and added, "Unless you act like an asshole."

We smiled at the shared awareness of that possibility

It would be days and only while Bob was asleep and he and I were alone in the room that I trained my sight on his wound and was appalled to find the red, puckered kiss of a slightly open mouth in the wrong place.

I sat down to still the dizziness and told myself to do this whenever he was asleep, so that when he wasn't, I could do so without repugnance. Once he was out of the hospital, I would be removing, emptying, and changing the pouches, cleaning that wound.

My poor husband, my ardent lover.

Seducing the Nurses

THREE MONTHS AGO WE'D BEEN SAILING. Just a couple of weeks ago we were fattening Bob for chemotherapy. And now I was seducing the hospital nurses. I had to win them over so Bob would receive attentive care. It was a challenge. They played hard to get.

They were over-worked; they didn't look up from their computers. Eye contact was minimal.

"What a great haircut! Where did you have it done?"

"We're going out for something to eat. What may we bring you?"

"These flowers were just sent. I'd like you to have them."

I was whoring for my husband's care.

A friend told me, "When my grandmother was in the hospital, we always kept food in the room and let the nurses know it was there, inviting them to help themselves."

When I came home at night exhausted by the weight of sorrow permeating Bob's floor, I rallied the strength to make brownies for the next day's delivery. Chuck and Rebecca made chocolate chip cookies and bought boxes of Clementines. It was like feeding the birds. They don't come the moment you put up a feeder. They have to discover it's there before the flocks arrive. Finches, nuthatches, chickadees.

We family members of patients recognized one another by our pleas for attention, our lost awareness of day and night and by our weariness. We were all exhausted. Energy was sucked out of me the moment I walked off the street and through the hospital door.

That place was an industrial size vacuum cleaner, a soul sucker. We longed to crawl into any vacant bed. Just a little shot of that morphine, please. Sleep. We all wanted sleep. But it failed to come to those watching life leak out of their beloveds. We drank the cafeteria's watery coffee and read People Magazine. What were the royals up to? We rearranged the flowers. We listened to the beep of the intercom, the static filled voices. One person's news was everyone's news. We stared at machines registering blood pressure and heart rate. We went into the zone.

The nurses were in the nurse zone. Administer the meds. Enter the charts on the computers. Keep your head down, keep going. I wanted better for Bob and he was in no state to be seductive himself. For those over seventy, the side effects of anesthesia can be brutal. Some report paranoia, some hallucinations. Bob was cranky. No, he was not one of those guys about whom the nurses would say, "Oh, we all love Dr. Ascher." And so, the job fell to me to continue luring them into his room.

On the fourth day, something cracked. I went from seductress to lioness.

A resident entered Bob's room, sat on his bed and said, "So, how are you doing, Robert?" I wanted to answer, "Still dying." But, instead said, "Dr. Ascher. And please don't sit on his bed."

A few hours later, released from the rigors of their day, three doctors stopped to talk outside Bob's open door. They were laughing, easing into respite at shift's end. They started telling jokes. More laughter. Louder and more frequent. I stormed out and assuming them to be interns or residents, I seethed, "If you are training to be doctors, then you must learn some common courtesy. My husband is in there dying and recovering from the pain and shock of an ileostomy. Have some regard for the necessary privacy and quiet." Like grammar schoolboys they looked down at their shoes. "I'm sorry," murmured one. "You should be," I said. Kick 'em while they're down. Who says, "You should be" in response to an apology? Cruel mothers and crazed wives.

And where was that voice coming from? I tended to follow my father's adage; "You catch more flies with honey than vinegar." My father the diplomatic headmaster would never tell a group of doctors to mind their manners. No, he would go to that door and say, "What do you say, old sports, how about moving down the hall a bit?" He would smile. His jaw would be clenched. But he would smile. And they would move. Believe me, they would move.

Later, a friend at the hospital told me that one of the physicians I'd scolded was a big deal. The head of a department.

"Good," said I. He shook his head. I didn't care. My job was to protect my injured one. Unless you had his best interests in mind, you weren't welcome.

And Yet…

THERE WERE MOMENTS when I sensed I was visited by miracle in that place of glaring lights, fear and squeaky, rubber soled shoes.

Winnie walked into our lives and would change the course of both sickness and death. Not in curing but in loving.

I'd hit the skids. Sleep deprivation sent me to the private duty nurses' office seeking someone to stay with Bob at night. Medicare wouldn't pay, I was told. This would be out of pocket. "Fine." The overwhelming medical bills that had begun to pile up seemed irrelevant compared to Bob's comfort. The anxiety over the lack of funds would not hit until later, when all went silent and there was no more Bob. For now, I wanted him to have a private nurse's aide. Whatever it took. "Please send somebody kind."

The first night did not go well. When I arrived in the morning, Bob said, "No. Not her again." Done. I asked for someone else. This morning I walked in to find a smiling husband. "Now Winnie," he said, gesturing to her, "She's an angel."

So, Winnie it was night after night. She came to him after her day job in the operating room. She filled his darkened room with her large presence, her cheer, stories and goodness.

She was from Mandeville, a small town in the hills of Jamaica. A friend who grew up there told me, "It's a place of eccentric characters and unusual occurrences," where boundaries between what is deemed "real" and imagined are fluid. She said, "Angels live there. Winnie's not the first."

She and Bob quickly loved each other and talked late into the nights.

He listened as she told him about her life as the sole supporter of her children and grandchildren. On days off she cooked for the week ahead — sometimes for her entire Queens neighborhood. Curries, roti, ribs, jerk chicken all spread out on tables in her back yard. Her youngest son would hand out flyers announcing an upcoming all-you-can-eat event at Winnie's. Free of charge.

Bob's contribution to their nocturnal dialogues was to advise against spoiling the children, working too hard, failing to demand the respect she deserved. In exchange, she told him about Jesus and the power of prayer. About the music in her church where she was an usher every Sunday. She gave us the number for dial-a-prayer.

When did she sleep? I began to worry about and fuss over her. We were all falling in love and determined to keep her on until the end. Yes, I thought like this. The end.

I'd been keeping a sharp lookout for signs and wonders, for beneficence leaking into the horror. Winnie was our first wonder. There were to be many.

Alive

TEN DAYS LATER BOB CAME HOME, and we began to experience an inexplicable intensity of being alive.

Surgery and a ready supply of pain medication had eased his alarming, physical symptoms. And in spite of brittle fatigue, we seemed to be vibrating with life. I had noted this phenomenon in the '80s at a center for AIDS patients for whom I cooked lunch. They lived with all senses sharpened and saturated. "Barbara, this is a symphony," one once commented upon taking a bite of chili. When asked why another didn't use the dishwasher as we cleaned up after serving thirty young men, he plunged his hands deep into the sink's hot, soapy water and said, "Because I want to know I'm washing dishes." The pain they suffered was secondary to the power of life. Bob and I had entered a similar state of being.

This is why men love war, according to Bill Broyles' 1984 *Esquire* article, "Part of the love of war stems from its being an experience of great intensity... [It] replaces the difficult gray areas of daily life with an eerie, serene clarity."

Similarly, according to a reporter's account of the blitz, the citizens of London were "pulsating with life."

So were we. We felt the pulse within and around us. There was gleeful laughter, an illuminated awareness of the boundlessness of our love, luminous moments of clarity and appreciation. All the bullshit of life had been blown away as if by the winter wind rattling our windowpanes. What remained was a quiet calm into which this delight, gratitude, and occasional jubilation flowed. I felt something akin to elation when biting into my sister Becky's delivery of still warm gingerbread with homemade sabayon sauce and sautéed apples.

And this morning, I was stunned by what can only be described as an interlude of ecstasy. Last night was one of bursting ileostomy bags, which had necessitated cleaning the wall, the bed, my husband and attaching new bags over the open-mouthed wound. A major source of Bob's happiness had always been taking care of me and being my exquisite lover. Now his powerlessness resulted in ongoing apology. "Barbar, I'm sorry but the bag has burst again."

Last night was a series of such apologies. Now, as I stood at the kitchen counter preparing to squeeze our breakfast orange juice, I could barely feel my feet, my brain was stuck on pause. Pause with static. I sliced the fruit and put each half into Bob's mother's 1920's, heavy iron, hand press. As I pushed the handle down, a sense of euphoria bubbled up in me like percolating coffee. One of Wordsworth's "fleeting moods/Of shadowy exultation..."

I brought the juice into the dining room where Bob sat reading the paper. "The strangest thing just happened," I described the experience. "Yes," said he, "This has been a time of great joy as well as suffering."

Perhaps we were experiencing one of Flannery Connor's "mercies." Suffering from lupus and facing its dismal prognosis, she noted, "Sickness before death is a very appropriate thing and I think those who don't have it miss one of God's mercies." This would have mystified me in the past. We can listen and read and read and read but there are aspects of being human for which we cannot prepare until we have direct experience. Until we're in the thick of it. Our love was revealing itself in new ways as we protected and cosseted each other in this calm, in T.S. Eliot's "lucid stillness." We were vibrantly present, aware and quiet.

This would not be the first or last time we felt touched by grace. One would think, given the degree of our adoration of and dependence upon each other, we would be anguished. We were not. We had a job to do… bidding each other farewell. And we would bring all our love to bear in that process.

Over breakfast we laughed when I reminded him of O'Connor's far from funny short story; "A Good Man is Hard to Find." A murderer, identified as The Misfit kills a "foolish old woman" who, with his gun to her head has a flash of discernment. The deed done, her killer thinks, "She would have been a good woman if she'd of only had someone to shoot her every day of her life."

Having a gun pointed at our heads inspired us to become our best, most open hearted, honest and bravest selves. Alternate states like this don't occur as acts of volition. They are there when we've been stripped of incidentals. There were many times when we felt blessed. It was as though certain death had granted us an extra life.

Sorrow and despair can shut us down or as I was learning by Bob's bedside, it can open us to something clear, vital and true. Call it love.

Of course, Broyles "difficult gray areas of daily life" intruded. This wasn't war. My mother called to say that unlike the previous two years, she wasn't coming for Christmas. "Why, Ma? It's going to be a tough one. It would be so nice to have you here." She started to cry, but not for me. "Because it would be too painful. What you and Bob are going through is just bringing it all back to me." "It" referred to my father's illness and swift demised.

"Well, whatever you want." I thought but did not say to this woman grown fragile in widowhood, "I want a mother by my side."

I didn't say it because it had never been our way. I didn't say it because it would have been too painful to hear her respond, "No." Ours was a relationship of evasion motivated by fear of imagined hurt inflicted by the spoken rather than implied word. I didn't say, "I need you," because she'd tell me, "You're making me feel guilty." That would deliver us to the long song and dance of a life-time, "Don't feel guilty. It's alright." I learned long ago that to wish for a different relationship was to go down the path of despair and so at an early age became fiercely independent.

I hung up and reported the conversation to Bob who laughed it away. "Why are you surprised?" He knew she wouldn't show up for me. Not this Christmas, not in the days to come. She was too overwhelmed by her own emotions to make room for mine. She lived two and a half hours from here but had made no appearance.

"You're right." I kissed him. In our life together he had often been the voice of reason and humor when familial matters brought me down. His response to, "Why does she do that?" "Why does he say that?" was often to remind me that family members were who they were and, "They're doing the best they can do." This acceptance had allowed him to forgive his own parents, Charles and Helen, their far more egregious parental carelessness. As young marrieds in the '20s and '30s they were gorgeous, in demand "New York intellectuals."

It was the latter that motivated residents of the Barn House, a summer commune on Martha's Vineyard to request them as their "Summer Intellectuals." Room and board in exchange for being brilliant and scintillating at meals served in the Barn. Yes, they were compelling. Charles of the five languages and a mind that encompassed legions. Helen, of the beauty and charm irresistible to men. What they were not was adequate to the demands of raising a child. Not narcissists' strong point.

Following that Barn House summer, the Ascher family spent every June to September in rented homes "Up Island," where artists, activists and liberals joined the year round population of fishermen. They talked long and late at dinner parties and continued the conversation without clothes every sunny day on Roger Baldwin's beach. It was hard to imagine serious considerations of pressing, world issues with breasts in your face. Or for a little boy to concentrate on building a sand castle while Max Eastman crouched wide legged to comment on its progress. The parents' attempts to convey that this-is-all-natural were wasted on their young son who didn't especially want to see the grown-ups' genitalia.

By the time he was eight, Bob had found a means of escape. A retired whaling captain helped him build a sailboat. From then on, he was on his own, sometimes for days at a time, staying with the caretakers of Nashawena Island across the sound. This raised no alarms. Helen was engaged in love affairs and liberal causes. Once while sitting on Menemsha Beach with friends who watched her little boy in a ten-foot boat heading out the channel, they asked, "Aren't you worried?" "Why?" was her reply? "He always comes back."

Charles was absent, working in the city. He was the parent I knew, Helen having predeceased him, and the only way to connect with him was through the frontal lobe. Foreign affairs, art, and opera, these were the interests of his heart yet when speaking of them his voice was a level drone devoid of emotion. He was mystified by and dismissive of his passionate, fiery son.

At sixteen, when afflicted with rheumatic fever for the second time, Bob was sent to live alone in Arizona for a year. Pre-penicillin, it was an ominous disease and he'd been warned of potential heart damage. That early exposure to a dread disease had made him believe that his life would be short.

Living alone in a rented house he was occasionally visited by a family friend who gave him a gun "to shoot rattle snakes," and advised to always shake out his boots before stepping into them. "Rattlers like to sleep in there." His mother visited once.

So much to forgive and yet he did. Of Charles, the aging widower to whom he was attentive, he explained to me, "Just because he can't be a good father, doesn't mean I can't be a good son."

He was right, none of us sets out determined to be a "bad" parent. We do the best we can with what we've got. My mother wasn't deliberately letting me down and though I was disappointed, her not showing up for Christmas was small in our scheme of things.

Life Interferes

THE FOLLOWING DAY, clouds obscured the previous day's light-filled orange juice elation. It's not in the nature of luminosity to stick around. Ask Shelley. It's always a good idea to ask Shelley. "Our best and happiest moments... arising unforeseen and departing unbidden." Pulsating life departed unbidden and was replaced by pulsating rage. Exhaustion can do that. As can being premenstrual and hard up. I was all of these. I threatened to stab the dog in the heart if he didn't stop pacing. I made certain to keep my dark mood far from Bob. I breathed deeply, I meditated before leaving our bedroom and going to him in the living room.

Above all else, I wanted to convey that I was o.k. and would be o.k. Doing fine, just fine. Will do fine.

But, once removed from him, I contemplated the absurdity of the facile, modern rage for "quality of life" and "good death." As if either had much to do with real life and real death.

Rebecca accompanied me to the pharmacist to fill another prescription. I sat down and she saw my tears. The first I'd shed since diagnosis. She knelt before me and took my hands. "Tell me Mom. I'm strong today and you'll help me when you are and I'm not."

I choked on the words. "What if I'm never touched again?"

She reached up and held me.

A visiting friend told me at the door and out of Bob's earshot, "I know a harpist who plays for terminal patients. It calms them." She offered to send for her. Ugh. Hokey. I held my tongue. Harp my ass. Death is cruel and messy. Anyone who walked through the door with a harp and a sweet smile would be shot between the eyes.

If I had a gun. If there were a harp.

I was resentful when the outside world banged on the door disturbing our intense intimacy. This morning it kept knocking.

The bank called. I was in danger of bouncing checks. I'd forgotten to make deposits.

The mortgage broker called. We missed the closing date for a lower interest rate.

At night I had examination dreams. Not only had I not studied; I hadn't attended one class all semester. Exactly. We were facing death and I hadn't gone to class.

New Year's Eve

A FRIEND ARRIVED FOR TEA. One in the constant flows of visitors who cheered Bob. He engaged them in lively, laughing conversation. When the children came from Cambridge and San Diego, he was gleeful. He told Ellen who arrived to take care of apartment details, and help her father, "You are everything a father could want in a daughter." So important, this interlude. Children need to hear this at all ages, but Ellen had been short-changed, sandwiched between a brother and sister dazzling in their beauty and inteligence. She had not been praised enough, singled out enough, listened to enough. But now, she heard those words and they stayed her.

These visits from the children, and in Lizzie and Steve's cases, their spouses, made him almost giddy. Their presence had power to overwhelm chemotherapy's related nausea and cancer's gnawing pain. He was happy. It reminded me of the times before all this that I'd requested we not answer the phone during dinner and he would respond, "But what if the kids call?" That was not something the older three did regularly, but Bob always hoped they would.

Every family has its narrative and each member his or her own. The children's is not mine to write. How can I know the effects of living in a home fraught with tension and unhappiness? How can I know the effects of divorce? For each of the three arriving with unique dispositions at various times in the family history, the story would be different. In general I would say, divorce sucks. Remarried parents may make attempts to salve their guilt by sharing newfound happiness, but does that assuage the pain of family dissolution? I think not. But again, this is conjecture. Lizzie had told me during the first year of Bob's and my marriage, "It's wonderful to see Dad so happy." But I couldn't imagine that held much sway for her, the child closest to her father. Adolescents by nature and necessity are self-absorbed. Was Lizzie's happiness for her father sustainable when their mother remarried a month after we did and moved with the children five hours away to a home inhabited by her new husband and his three children? How and why would Bob's happiness have offset the pain in that transition? And of the three, Lizzie had always been the one most change averse. She had always liked to stay put.

The other two suffered in their own way. Ellen held onto a hope that her parents would get back together. And Steve? In his stepfather, Bob Hulsizer he acquired a kind and thoughtful man who shared his love of sailing, something they would do together in the small, classic, wooden boat his father had given Steve. The two won many a victory in the weekly Menemsha Pond races. But his father wasn't around when there were issues yet to be resolved. In his film, Steve's doppelganger wished he'd asked his father, "Why couldn't we stay a family?" Yes, the complexity of family relationships is such that I would be doing the three older children a disservice by offering anything other than surmise.

Gabriel went out with a dog walker and I served visitors tea, crumpets and homemade strawberry preserves. Best cups. Two teapots, one with black, the other with herbal. Chocolate chip cookies. I was taking care of a dying man here. My standards were high.

The dog was returned with his body hunched in the shape of a bow. "He can't poop," the walker said. "He tried and tried but couldn't." The dog, too? What an absurd scene in an absurd place. It seemed that he might have intestinal obstruction.

"Gotta go to the vet." I asked a guest to stay with Bob then called the doorman to help me lift the dog no longer capable of standing. I ran to the garage, drove to the door of our apartment building, settled Gabriel onto the back seat, then careened down the FDR Drive to the Animal Medical Center, the same route I'd been speeding along for the past few weeks. A car full of pain. Gabriel's cries sounded like a child's. I wished he sounded more like a dog.

There was no one behind the desk in the cold, still lobby. Frantic, I considered getting on the elevator and going to any floor where I might find help. Shades of Bob in the emergency room. But, before I did, the security guard returned. Slowly. Very slowly.

"My dog is sick and I can't lift him out of the car."

He'd call for a vet but wasn't encouraging. "It's New Years Eve."

Well, I knew that.

Meanwhile Gabriel trembled and suffered alone. This was the season of trembles. "Please get a stretcher and help me."

He couldn't leave his post.

"But my car is right there," I pointed through the glass doors.

He got up with effort and reluctance to retrieve and wheel a cold, stainless steel gurney onto the street. I put my arms around Gabriel's front end so that he could see and smell me and asked the guard to pick up the rear as we move him.

Naturally, the brakes weren't on. There went Gabriel, rolling down to the East River. I ran, grabbed hold and by the time I pushed him back uphill and inside, a vet stood waiting. I wanted to throw my arms around her, to thank her for not being a party girl.

Upstairs, she palpated Gabriel's hard, distended belly and proclaimed him impacted. She stuck her finger up his rectum. "Ah, yes. Ah, yes, I think…" She tugged and pulled out a large, solid piece of feces. "This was blocking the rest." The rest came in a rush. Even she was overcome by the smell. I'd become accustomed to breathing through my mouth.

After the dash to deposit checks that morning, I'd boarded a 5th Ave. bus downtown for the celebration of the day — buying Bob a pair of elegant pajamas. Thin Man era pajamas. As I took a seat, my phone rang. It was Bob. "The damn bag is leaking,"

"I'll be right there." I got off the bus at 77th. "Quick trip," noted the driver. If she only knew. I had a bizarre desire to tell her the whole story.

Racing home, I found my husband surrounded by paper towels, struggling to press the ileostomy pouch to his side. He looked up, "I'm so sorry, Barbar. You shouldn't have to be seeing this." Apologetic stoicism, keeping his focus trained on me was his way of coping. He could tolerate the suffering. What he could not tolerate was mine.

I kissed the top of his head, took off my coat and changed the bag. Which is why, as the vet retrieved the dog's feces, I laughed. Puzzled, she looked at me. "Oh," I explained, "Just a cosmic joke. I spent the day dealing with shit."

Do You Remember the Man You Married?

OUR DEAR, STEADFAST FRIENDS Jeannette and Alex Sanger took me to the Metropolitan opera and dinner on the Mezzanine. I was astonished yet again by the power of the senses to survive duress and deliver joy. The taste of good food, the sound of exquisitely trained voices, the transporting sight of stage sets, the cold grip of air when we stepped into the clear, star sharp night.

The first special treat of the day had been reading the Sunday Times over a quiet breakfast at the neighborhood diner.

The waitress came to set the table, "Just one?" I nodded. I felt as though the air has been knocked out of me. "Yes. Just one."

Old habits steady us. Bob and I continued our evening ritual of reading poetry to each other over dessert. As always, each of us shared a favorite chosen from our library shelves. Last night, I'd read Stanley Kunitz' *The Testing Tree*. I was that boy, throwing the stone, wishing for luck, and like a child, believing in it. And like that boy, I was a scout looking for the trail. The only one I trusted these days was the trail of our love. My conviction was that following its well-worn path was the true way.

Bob read the same poet's, *Touch Me*. "Do you remember the man you married? / Touch me, remind me who I am." His voice caught. He held my hand. "No more poetry."

And so, no more poetry, no more music. No Chopin, Brahms, Prokoviev. Only the early Italians. We'd stick to the early Italians. I laughed and reminded him of the piece in the Times years earlier that described an annotated Boston Symphony program from the days when Brahms was considered modern. "Exit in case of Brahms."

I took his hand and said, "So, that's our deal. We'll exit in case of Brahms."

Chemo

SOMEDAY, IN HISTORICAL NOVELS, in movies about the 21st century, the audience will respond to depictions of chemotherapy as we do now when reading of medieval torture. The rack. The Pear of Anquish.

It was now impossible to tell which was causing the greatest distress, the cancer or its treatment. Lasix was prescribed for his legs' alarming swelling. The skin was stretched so taut it looked as though it might burst, no longer capable of containing what was within.

I offered possible ease of the chemo-induced nausea. "I'll buy you some pot. I think I might be able to get it through one of the bird watchers who's a stoner."

"No."

"Why? It will help with the nausea."

"Because it's illegal."

Huh? This man was sick and in pain yet considering legalities.

"When'd you become a goody-goody?"

I sat down with him, took his hand and said what had been on my mind for a week.

"Sweetheart. Are you sure you want to continue with this therapy? It seems so brutal. Is it really worth it?"

"Yes. If it means I have one more day with you."

When I asked the doctor the same question and told him that Bob's suffering was breaking my heart, he said, "Yes, but if we stop it will break his."

Going Home to Die

THREE WEEKS AFTER THE NEW YEAR, we returned to the hospital for treatment of further complications.

He grew weaker and thinner. Odd expression, to grow weak. To grow thin. I was becoming a stranger to my own language. How could it not seem absurd since it was absurdly inadequate to the circumstances?

"He knows what's going on," Winnie told me. "He knows that whatever he takes in goes right out."

We both knew but did not speak of it. So what. He was going to die and was wasting away. What was there to say?

I made certain that everything that crossed his tongue delighted his palate. Pleasure was more important than nutrition. "You want me to make you an apple pie?" Yes. Oh, yes, please.

The doctors were intent on keeping him in the hospital. They contended there were procedures that could only be done there. "Like what?" I asked.

"Administering I.V. fluids. Pain management." I didn't buy it. Especially the latter. Perhaps a Pain Team seemed a good idea to the corporate board. "Pain management" had become part of the lingo not the reality. For days the "Pain Team" failed to respond in spite of repeated calls. When they appeared, they nodded their heads to make up for the emptiness of their hands. At home, I could do better with vodka and oxycodone. I knew we were nearing the end and I was determined that this was not the place Bob would die. My 95-year-old Buddhist friend Margot Wilkie said, "Hospitals are so depriving of death." And so depriving of life.

I asked for a meeting with Bob's medical team, the surgeon, oncologist, and David. We stood in the hall and I told them, this time with conviction, with a new confidence that I was in charge and could insist, "I want to take my husband home."

"You can't."

They repeated the reasons and, "He needs regular injections of Demerol."

"I can do that."

No. They were insistent until I said with force and certainty, "I am taking my husband home to die."

Stricken silence. They looked as though they couldn't get away from me fast enough. It was as though that word had cast a curse.

"You can teach me how to give a shot. Chuck can manage the I.V. We're going home."

Arrangements were made. The oncologist invited me to come to his office the next morning. He'd teach me how to give an injection to an orange.

A Double Life

AND SO, ON FRIDAY, almost three months since diagnosis, I brought Bob home for the second and last time, bed to wheelchair, wheelchair to car and then car to wheelchair, wheelchair to apartment, the last time Bob would go through that door alive. We brought Winnie with us to help with the move. We'd asked and she'd agreed to return and spend nights whenever I was in need of sleep. The privilege of being able to do this was not lost on me. How many were unable to die at home because there was no support? Too many. Way too many. Nothing about medical care was fair, just and equal.

I slept next to him on the pull-out couch next to the hospital bed we'd set up in the dining area, the center of domestic life between kitchen and living room, the most frequented route assuring he would rarely be without company, a passing chat, a kiss. From there, he could see visitors come in the front door. He could see the children, Chuck and I moving from one room to another. You couldn't get there without passing through here.

It was around this bed that spontaneous, nightly theme parties commenced. This first night, I got out of bed to inspect the source of laughter coming from the living room and found Bob sitting in the chair next to his bed, a cold, wet washcloth on his head. "Steve taught me how to do this," he said. A treatment for fever, pain, whatever ailed. He was nodding to the beat of the reggae disc Winnie was playing

Sitting cross legged on the floor was Tshering, a delicate, innately gracious, quiet young Tibetan woman who'd come to live with us soon after diagnosis. Her duties were to take care of household matters so I could take care of Bob without distraction. I'd hired her without an interview. There'd been no time after the first crisis. I'd asked members of my Buddhist group with whom I'd been meditating for six years, if they knew of anyone who could do this job and not be intrusive? One responded, "I was trekking in Nepal last summer with a wonderful, young woman who I think is living in New Haven." She'd track her down. The next day she did and I called. Could she move in tomorrow? I relied on the response. "Yes."

Her own family had banished her because she was living with and planning to marry a young man of a different cast. Bob filled the void, supporting her decision to go with love in spite of the odds. He knew that odds tested love and if it survived, then it was worth fighting for. There was no time for instructions, but wise beyond her 21 years, she intuited what had to be done. She observed how the household worked and was so bright, observant and compassionate that within a week she was making nourishing soups easy to digest for two people lacking appetites.

She cut Bob's toenails when she noted he couldn't bend over to do it himself. She massaged his feet. She walked the dog and ran errands relieving me from having to leave Bob's side. We loved this young woman who had arrived a stranger and quickly became a steady source of comfort and support. Rebecca sat on his bed. It was as if she and I had been born to this. Even as a young girl, the realization that she had an"older" father had never been far from her mind We had accepted this possible fate long ago and now we would do what we'd set out to do the moment of diagnosis, focus all our love on this husband, this father. Chuck untangled I.V. lines, smiling as he did so.

Large-Hearted-Winnie sat on a stool in the midst of it all, telling a story about the night she got stoned with Bob Marley. Everyone was laughing so hard, Rebecca had tears streaming down her face.

There was nothing for it but to make rum punch. No matter the hour. I brought out the best pitcher, the cut glass one almost too heavy to lift, too precious to risk breaking. The one saved "for good." Ridiculous. I squeezed fresh limes and oranges, added dark rum and a dash of Triple Sec, stirred in sugar and ice, too bad we didn't have maraschino cherries. I put it all onto a tray and we were off.

Chuck and I joined Rebecca on Bob's bed, raised our glasses and toasted the day, each other, the drink itself. The party went through the night and into the early hours.

For this is the day you have been given. Rejoice and be glad in it.

The following night, heartened by our enthusiasm for all things Marley, Winnie showed up with jerk chicken, pork, roti and her Marley C.D.'s. We searched the back and bottom of my drawers for old tie-dye tee shirts. No luck, so I borrowed mine from Emily, my five-year-old neighbor who'd just made one in school.

Out came the Red Stripe beer, pop, pop, pop, and Winnie began to dance. She tried to teach us white girls how to move. It was useless. We followed the waves of her floating, flowing motion. Our butts weren't made for such grace. Bob requested that we raise the volume and once we had, he picked up the weights kept nearby and lifted them to the beat. I knew I would never forget his grin. There was something about this dying that filled the air with energy. We felt as though we could dance forever.

The following night was White Nights celebrated with Stoli frozen to a sticky consistency. As though feeding a bird, I placed Caspian Sea caviar on Bob's tongue. He delighted in the flavors, the slippery, wet orb that gave to the bite and released the sea. He smoked with guilt free gusto. What was there to lose? Perhaps we live most intensely, most vibrantly when there's nothing to lose.

In spite of the moratorium on poetry, in keeping with the Russian theme, I considered reading Joseph Brodsky's poems, then determined them too laden with exile. We were home exactly as we'd fought to be and would be exiled soon enough.

Instead, I followed Tess Gallagher's and Raymond Carver's example. During his final illness she read him a Chekhov short story every day. I removed *Early Short Stories* from the shelf and found what I was looking for — "Joy." Back by Bob's side, I curled up on the chair and began to read. We both reveled in the author's sense of the absurd. The odd things that bring us joy. Its illusory quality.

Learning of our nocturnal revels, a Hawaiian friend sent an overnight shipment of leis shimmering with fragrant jasmine, tuberose, plumeria and orchids smaller than an infant's thumbnail. Grass skirts, a garish Hawaiian shirt for Bob and music to inspire hulas. More life! More life!

I made Mai Tais based on some ancient memory of a misbegotten, teenage night at Trader Vic's. We ate strips of fresh pineapple but skipped roasting a pig on a spit, having neither an open fire nor the heart to rotate a small animal over it.

Saturday came; Winnie was at home and the children out. I announced, "Tonight's theme is, 'Happily Married Couple Dines at Home Alone.'"

"Thank God!" Bob sighed and smiled.

Although we know there is no turning back death, the antidote isn't limited to its arrest, but exists in celebrating life's moments remembered and experienced. A double life. Menemsha sunsets were as present as the moon that rose that night. We were not in denial; we knew we were close to the end. We were not feigning cheer for one another, friends or the children. We had our fingers on the strong, beating pulse of that old, insistent passion.

It was as though these past few days had been Bob' entire life condensed, refined and shining bright. So much joy. So much love and wisdom. In the time left to us, we would continue to laugh, sing and dance around a hospital bed, being careful not to trip over I.V. tubes in this profoundly altered home, this place that had held our life.

Pajama Party

REBECCA AND CHUCK INVITED ME out for dinner. "You need a break." I didn't want to leave. I wanted, as Genesis would have it, to "cleave unto" Bob. Anticipatory separation set in.

They insisted. Bob urged, "Go."

They knew a great bistro in the Village. Too far, too far, I thought but wanted to please them by allowing them the opportunity to please me. They also needed a break. Every night following his last surgical case Chuck had been showing up to change I.V. bags and tend to any other medical needs that had arisen that day. His mere presence provided what was needed most — love, cheer and security. His affability didn't waiver and unlike the rest of us he never exhibited symptoms of exhaustion.

Rebecca extended her leave of absence from work in order to be here full time. Yesterday when I returned to the apartment after filling a prescription, I found her sitting on the floor next to her father cleaning the opening in his side and replacing the pouch. As they conversed with their habitual ease, one could have mistaken the moment as ordinary. What wasn't ordinary was Bob's acceptance of this role reversal. He had stood by her bed through appendicitis, juvenile rheumatoid arthritis, kidney infections. His arrival and hand holding made everything seem less painful, less frightening. I had also experienced the power of his presence to heal or make that seem a possibility. Through flu and various visiting viruses, he would sit on the bed with one hand on mine, the other on my forehead. There was something soothing about his long fingers, about his intense gaze willing me to get better.

I was frightened imagining the first illness to be endured without him. But now, he was the passive one, a state that would have once enraged him did not. He'd accepted the ultimate passivity. He'd done what could be done to delay death and now there was nothing more to do.

"Great," I said. It was decided. We got into our coats, I kissed Bob goodbye. As Chuck drove us downtown, I kept thinking, too much distance. Too much distance between me and his side.

The restaurant was full. There would be an hour's wait. No, we agreed to go somewhere else. They knew a place nearby that had pretty good food and entertainment provided by drag queens.

I couldn't eat. I couldn't pay attention to the show. I understood that this was meant to distract and lighten. But, I said, "I love you both so much and thank you for doing this for me, but I have to go home."

Once there, I found Bob sitting in his chair and as usual, laughing with Winnie. Love had taught him how to live and now how to die. He had retained enough strength to live the end of his life. I climbed onto his bed and told him where we'd been and how we ended up there. Amused and incredulous he asked, "You left me for drag queens?"

Hours passed into deeper and deeper night and we remained as engaged as a couple newly in love out on a date. We talked and talked and talked and laughed.

"Curfew," I declared at two in the morning. "We should both get some sleep. I'm going to give you a shot of Demerol."

"No."

"Why not?"

"I don't want to be drugged."

"Well, I do."

"Winnie, give her one of my fentanyl lollipops. She needs sleep."

She obliged and I went to bed with sweet, red candy in my

mouth. I didn't sleep. I spent the night staring up at and dancing on the ceiling.

When the light came in our east window and my mind allowed my body to come down onto the bed, I got up to greet Bob. But he was asleep. At last, thank goodness. Winnie said they had continued to talk for a long time after I retired and he closed his eyes. As I leaned over to kiss his forehead he didn't stir. Something was different.

Hand Holding Chair

HE FAILED TO AWAKEN THAT DAY. I informed the three older children, who'd been in and out, taking time from work and family to travel here as often as possible. Arriving, they commenced to set up camp in the living room. "It's the Paint Box all over again," said Steve, referring to our tiny, summer, rental shack where for years we'd shared one bathroom and little privacy. .

I pointed to the chair next to Bob's bed. "This is the hand holding chair. Please make sure somebody's in it, 24/7."

Whenever Chuck came, he sat there talking into Bob's sleep. He told him about his last case; about a trip he and Rebecca were planning, about their dog.

We all took turns holding his hand, kissing his brow, whispering words of love.

I had heard that even in a coma, a patient responds to touch and sound. I decided he might still appreciate taste, so occasionally swabbed the inside of his mouth with vodka or a fine, well-aged single malt Scotch. I sang to him.

"How much do I love you?
I'll tell you no lie
How deep is the ocean..."

I'd sung that for him at his birthday party last spring.

Odd that birthday. He hadn't wanted the party. "Why? It's a no-account birthday. Why don't you wait for my 80th?"

"Tough. I've already booked the library at the Cosmopolitan Club."

I sent invitations to forty friends. Cocktails and music 6 to 8, March 12th.

Where had that stubborn refusal to oblige come from? It was not in my nature to turn a deaf ear to his protestations, to forge ahead with plans in spite of them. We know so much more than we think we know. So much more than standard evidence would support.

I practiced that song until I could hit the high note on "cry," ("And if I ever lost you, how much would I cry?")

He was the one to cry as I stood at the piano and sang, never shifting my gaze from his. Carolyn Mackenzie, whom Rebecca always referred to as "your pretty friend Carolyn Mackenzie," kept her arm around his shoulders. At the end, he crossed the room and held me tight. How deep is the ocean?

And so, kneeling next to the bed and resting my head on his chest, I began to sing to him and faltered. "No. I'm not going to sing that one, it's too sad." I hoped he hadn't heard my voice break.

Days went by. He slept through Monday, Tuesday and Wednesday when we all agreed that Chuck could disconnect the I.V. fluids. Everyday Margot Wilkie sat discretely meditating at the far end of the living room. Fifty years of Buddhist practice rendered her a steadying and reassuring presence.

I'd met her twenty-five years ago when at my request, Jeannette Sanger sat us together at a dinner party. I'd been mesmerized by her for years, watching her at parties. She was striking in her regal bearing, white hair and blue eyes that fixed on the person with whom she spoke. People were drawn to her and she to them.

Bob was equally attracted to the then 80-year-old Margot and found her sexy as it seemed all men did, judging from the crowd always gathered around her. Something to remember when I'm old, I told myself. It's not all about a cute butt.

Some people are like that. It's as though there is an invisible thread connecting you and all that's required is to pull it in. And so, I asked hostesses of various parties to introduce me. Again and again. After numerous, futile requests, I realized those who knew her guarded their access jealously. When one of them told me that she was a Buddhist, I was determined to meet her in spite of that resistance.

After my brother Bobby died at the age of 31, and I failed to find solace or guidance in my traditional, Western, religious beliefs, after talking to thoughtful and responsive Catholic, Episcopal, Unitarian and Presbyterian religious leaders, always asking the same question. Why AIDS? Why suffering? After a week's retreat at an Episcopal Monastery in upstate New York where I shook my fist at God and joined the monks in silence, I realized I needed another way, an additional way to explore the subject of suffering. And thus began my beginner's study of Buddhism and the Buddha's central tenant that suffering is inevitable but not incurable. I wanted to know more.

Jeannette Sanger took care of that by introducing me to Margot. Jeannette a generous friend had been taking care of things since I first knew her in college. She had the knack of being there if I needed her. When Bob was in the hospital, she showed up every day delivering sandwiches. Extravagant, crustless sandwiches from a purveyor to Old New York hostess's tea parties. Once he was home, she would arrive and say, "Give me a job." A demand more useful than the standard question, "Tell me if there's anything I can do to help," which puts the onus on one already overwhelmed. I don't know, I don't know. Make him well? Make me sleep? No. Hers was a simple command. Today, I took her into my office and asked, "Would you mind finding the least expensive funeral home? Tell them we want cremation and the ashes put into the simplest, least expensive box." She made the calls and a list.

Years ago, she had seated me next to Margot at a dinner party. I was struck by the older woman's wisdom that some attain in later life and was intrigued by her youthful energy and beauty that lent her a sense of agelessness.

"I understand you have a Buddhist group," I ventured midway through the first course. I'd heard that on Thursdays, a small group of eight women met in her living room one afternoon a week to meditate and discuss books on Buddhism. Occasionally she hosted a visiting Lama. In a nearly extinct, patrician, old money New York accent she acknowledged the gatherings. She told me that fifty years ago, she and her sister–in–law, Anne Morrow Lindbergh invited friends interested in reading about and discussing world religions to join them for weekly meetings at the Cosmopolitan Club. The focus turned to Tibetan Buddhism once Margot had met her teacher, Domo Geshe Rinpoche, a Tibetan monk and physician, recently escaped from years of imprisonment in a Chinese pigpen. He'd been spirited first to Dharamsala, then upstate New York. She would study with him until his death in 2001 and he would change the course of her life as he did for those of us lucky enough to meet him and know Margot.

Her story emboldened me to ask if I could become a member of the group?

She was silent before looking at me with her almost turquoise blue eyes. "What is it you would want to get out of such a group?" Her seriousness surprised me. It was clear that this wasn't like asking to join a book or opera group. Nor was it casual dinner party conversation. "Understanding," I said, "And wisdom."

She would call me. We would have to discuss this further.

That evening, I never noticed the others at the round table for eight. I knew better than to ignore the man on my left. I knew that before dessert, I was supposed to turn to him and ask a question, invite him into the conversation. I knew better but I didn't want to turn from Margot. I felt settled in a subtle new way. There was an easing of an old, nagging, occasional sense of being uncomfortable in my own skin.

By the time Bob remained asleep for two days, confusion and

impatience set in. Why, the children wanted to know, was it taking so long? There comes a time when you want relief from the tension. When anticipation becomes a reality, you imagine that at least there's something solid with which to cope. "If he doesn't die soon, I'm going to kill him," one of them said to laughter. The wait reminded me of the last week of pregnancy. Impatience followed by the pain.

My confidence began to waver. What we were doing felt right but what if it wasn't? I called David Globus, but he'd left town to visit his brother. Having a friend as your doctor had its down sides. I assumed he was absent because he couldn't face this end. I called to explain the situation to Henry Earle, David's covering physician. Since his office was just a block away, I asked if he'd mind stopping by after hours to let us know if we were doing the right thing?

Meanwhile, I asked Steve to call hospice to ask if that was called for. I heard him say to the person at the other end, "That's what we're doing." We'd created our own hospice, able to do so medically because of Chuck's constancy and psychologically due to the support of the children's attendance.

The minute I opened the door to Dr. Earle's quiet knock, no noisy doorbell, I sensed his kindness. This was a man whose goodness was large enough to encompass the situation. Taking his coat, I explained how we'd been ministering to Bob. "By instinct, not manual. I'm beginning to fear this might not be enough."

He nodded in the direction of Bob's bed, "May I?" "Please do." He crossed the room and I removed myself to the couch.

When he rejoined me, I gestured for him to sit down. "I didn't listen to his heart because my stethoscope is too cold. But, it won't be much longer." Although this was the first time we had met, we settled into the silent companionship of intimates. These were intimate times.

He mused as much to himself as to me, "You've picked up where modern medicine leaves off." He paused. "What you're doing is wonderful."

I told him that following the Buddhist tradition I wanted to keep the body in the apartment for a few days after death. It takes time for the soul to leave. He took my hand and said, "Take as much time as you like. Call me whenever you want me to come and sign the death certificate." He explained that once that was done, "strangers would enter the sacred space the family has created." He would stall that intrusion.

"It reminds me of cruising on Sea Hound," Steve noted. Yes, all of us stuffed onto our 26-foot sailboat, heading out of a harbor. A solid crew.

One of these original three, put their arms around me and said, "You're ours forever. You know that, right?"

Right. And they were mine. We had loved each other a long, long time.

The Bells Chime

WHEN NIGHT FELL, something started happening to my body or perhaps more aptly, something took over my body. Ferocity of pain in the gut made it impossible to walk to Bob's bedside where the others maintained their vigil.

A friend arrived, sat on the end of my bed and said, "Perhaps this is as it should be. It's said that the dying can't let go until the person with whom they are closely bound leaves the room."

"But I've been doing everything to assure him that we'll be okay, that he's free to go. I've told him his patients' bills were sent out. I've told him I've balanced the bank account..."

I struggled to the bathroom and blood poured out of me. I feared I was dying with Bob until I understood that my body had begun its mourning. I was shedding blood before tears.

In the hazy realm between sleep and consciousness, I heard the ship's clock on Bob's dressing room wall chime seven bells. 11:30. Jeannie, Steve's wife came into the room, "Barbie." I was too tired to open my eyes and she left. I knew why she'd come. Seven bells were the traditional death knell rung from medieval, English churches and monasteries. Nine bells announced the death of a woman. Seven for a man. She returned within the minute and sounded less tentative. "Barbie."

She walked to the bed and helped me up. "Can you walk?" I attempted it and got as far as the living room door, but the pain somewhere between the navel and below the breasts forced me to crawl the rest of the way. Months later, when I paid a visit to an acupuncturist and pointed to the source of distress, she would tell me, "That's the heart."

A deep, palpable peace had settled in the room.

I sat down in the hand holding chair. Silence. "Is it alright to touch him?" Jeannie asked.

I nodded even though in Buddhism the body is not to be touched until a monk or nun recites the required prayers. But, the Buddha also taught compassion. I was not going to tell family members how to respond to this moment. "Yes."

Winnie held his hand, Tshering wept as she held his feet placing her forehead on them in prayer.

I gazed in awe. He was there but not. He was Bob but not. It was as though he'd simply sailed away from his mooring.

As I stared into his face, I suddenly felt like a launched missile without a target. With striking clarity, I knew that it wasn't being loved I would miss as much as loving. What was I to do with all my love?

I went into the kitchen to call Jigme Rinpoche, one of my earliest Tibetan Buddhist teachers who had "happened" to arrive from his monastery in France a few days ago and had told me that if I called when Bob died, he'd come immediately. It was midnight and his sleepy attendant answered. I explained. He'd be right there.

Rinpoche was as responsible as Margot in bringing me to Buddhism. Before I knew anything, before I had met a lama, he and his brother, Sharma Rinpoche came to one of our Thursday teas at Margot's. As nine of us sat at the large, polished mahogany dining table, Margot's favorite gathering place for friends, I had asked them about their lives. "All of our family was killed." "We escaped from Tibet." All the while, in spite of the horror of their words, the merriness in their eyes didn't darken. This quality inspired me to tell Margot after they left, "Whoever they were, whatever they are, that's what I that."

And thus, I'd been set on the path. Little did I realize how much I would need "that," and in spite of years of practice, how little I had attained of such lightness of being.

Rebecca, smiling and shedding tears joined me in the kitchen and gave me a high five.

"We did it!" Triumphant. My girl's heart had not yet splintered. That was to come, but for now we celebrated that we'd accomplished what we'd set out to do.

In the past three months, we honored Bob as he had honored us. We redirected the love he had always poured forth. We erected a dam to send its unstoppable flow back to its source. Anyone who dived into those waters would drown. And that was our point. To drown him in the mighty power of love. Neither of us had ever experienced such directed, strong, focused, intense determination.

If there is any such thing as a "good death," we believed we had made that possible for this man we adored.

"How did you know he'd died?" I asked.

"Winnie was holding his hand and said, 'Something like an electric charge just went up my arm. That's the soul leaving. He's gone.' " The family standing around hadn't noticed as he slipped from one mystery into the next. The change was that silent, that gentle.

Rinpoche arrived, walked to Bob's bed, stood over him, then sat and began an almost inaudible chant.

Once he left and the family headed to various beds, I asked Winnie, "Will you please sit vigil?" I sensed the custom would not be foreign to her. It was not. "And Tshering, will you sleep on the pullout couch?" She would, but in the middle of the night, she crawled into my bed. "I've never slept in the same room as a dead person." I took her into my arms.

The next morning Rebecca called laughing. This is how it would go. Laughter, tears and back again. "Mom, this whole time we all thought you knew what you were doing and so, followed your lead. But, I just realized, you were making it up as you went along." Yes, I was, and bless the children for going along with it.

No, I'd never done "it," but hadn't felt like a novice.

Her moment of levity had died by nighttime and around midnight she arrived at the apartment to sleep next to me. This bed was becoming a subway turnstile. So many goings and comings. We needed to be close, to press our loss side to side. Especially at night when distractions faded away and the abyss opened.

At dawn, I slipped out of bed, dressed and walked around the corner to Bob's office. Once there, I opened the bedroom closet where he kept his bags of nautical gear. I reached into one and retrieved the pennants frayed around the edges from years of flying from the mast. This is what I'd come for.

Bob had been a follower of sailing protocol and knew when to raise a particular pennant and when to take it down. He knew to fly the American flag off the stern. To take it in and furl it at night. These rituals were among the children's duties.

Here was the owner's pennant, blue with a likeness of his yellow lab. The collar held five stars signifying his pre-Rebecca family and dog. I put various burgees on the blue rug about which there had been many discussions. Steve: "Do you like the blue rug?" Not particularly. Not that bright shade. Maybe he chose it because it reminded him of being on the water. Of a day to sail to Quicks Hole.

On those occasions, we'd be awakened by Bob declaring, "It's a beautiful day." Then he'd snap up the roller blinds in each bedroom. Snap, snap, snap followed by our groans. "Want to sail to Quicks?" What we'd wanted was to go back to sleep. But an hour later as we became coffee alert, there we were walking down to the harbor.

Lizzie was not a morning person, nor was her youngest sister. I was careful to put distance between myself and their dark glares, what Bob and I referred to as "storm clouds."

While he was dying, we had not planned what I had in mind. The most we had discussed was the memorial service. There came a moment when I wanted to know, "then what?" A month before the end, as I was cooking dinner and he was looking into the darkness outside the dining room window, listening to the familiar rattle of the street sign in the wind, I said, "I've been thinking. Would it be okay if we didn't scatter your ashes in the Cuttyhunk orchard? I know that's what we'd always talked about, but winter would be so desolate."

"Alright. Enough." Abrupt. Agreed but not to be mentioned again.

Sympathy and empathy have limits and when you reach them, you're stopped short and spun around as though driving a Dodge 'Em car of childhood fairs. Death brings us to that limit. I know we're all dying every day. I think about my own death. Cremation? Where to scatter the ashes? Will my beloveds want a place to visit and know that my bone chips are there? Such a place mattered to Bob and me after Bobby died. My parents' land on Cuttyhunk overlooked the harbor and Vineyard Sound. A bench was placed there beneath the choke cherry tree where his ashes had been buried. It was always our first stop when we sailed to the island, rowed to the dock and walked up the hill. This is where we sat remembering. When I was alone, I would talk to Bobby about missing him. I would apologize for not having been a better sister. Yes, it mattered. Who knows what is left behind along with ashes and bits of bone?

But imagining my own death didn't begin to take me to what Bob was experiencing. In this regard, I realized that for the first time, and in this way, he was a stranger to me. How could I know what it was like to face that he would soon leave this behind? His children, his wife, Bach, second chances?

In mentioning the locus of his eventual ashes, I'd ventured too close to the border of the terrain he had to travel alone. My ignorance raised a wall and I'd slammed into it. Enough. Push too hard and you'll be propelled in the opposite direction.

Back home from the office, I opened the window for a cold blast of February air and lined up the flags on the blanket covering his body. It seemed just right. Rebecca went downtown to buy incense and I put a sign on the door: "Please enter quietly. This is sacred space." Yes, Rebecca was right. I was making it up as I went along. And taking a big detour from Manhattan "edginess." Previously, I would not have pronounced this "sacred space" without a sense of irony.

Friends began to stop by, except for those who, upon hearing there was a body in the apartment, decided otherwise. Some of Rebecca's young friends apologized but confessed they were afraid of death. Some of ours remained standing in the foyer. Others who entered moved across the room to sit next to him. Later, I would discover prayers and poems they'd left beneath the bed.

So much of what I "made up" as I "went along," took no thought. It was as though an inner director had been telling me to enter stage right, exit stage left. Each movement seemed natural. Death and its approach take us to a place where instinct and intuition rule and self-consciousness is banished.

Second Goodbye

MY FRIEND AND NEIGHBOR Laura Palmer called. She had been one of the stalwarts who stood by all these months, arriving with offers of help and warm, homemade chocolate chip cookies and pies. "How are you this moment?" Silence. How could I say? She continued, "When my ex-husband died, the hardest part for me was seeing him taken away in a body bag." She wanted to spare me that and when the time came, would come to oversee the departure.

I told her, "I've scheduled the pickup for 2 a.m. when New York is at its quietest. I want the ride to be smooth and silent. I want peace at the end," This particular end.

When she arrived at one, she urged me back to bed. "You have got to get some sleep. I'll wake you before they leave." I obliged but sleep eluded me. How could it not? How could my body be other than on hyper-alert as the man who had been by my side and in my arms for thirty-five years was to be gone for good? Even though he had departed, he still took up space. Now, I was awaiting amputation. Giving up, I emerged to see two men in black suits and ties. Shadow men in my living room.

We shook hands. "Please take him down on the back elevator. And no body bag." They nodded. It was agreed.

I moved to Bob's bed and kissed the top of his head before putting on his favorite woolen cap. "To keep you warm," I whispered. For the same reason, I wrapped him in a soft blanket. He had always been sensitive to the cold.

As they moved his body from bed to gurney and headed for the door, I played Marley singing "Don't Worry Be Happy."

Bob left on a Reggae beat.

Ulysses Dog and Mine

THE NEXT MORNING, IT RAINED. Of course, it did. I stared out the kitchen window feeling an alien emptiness into which a throbbing ache began to seep.

"If I'm not reunited with Bob in the next life, I'll be really pissed," I told Tshering who had come to make tea. Later, when Margot called to check in and I repeated what I'd said to Tshering, she reassured, "You and Bob have been together for many lifetimes and will be again." I trusted her but, what if…? I worried that he would be reborn to a mother who wouldn't love him as I had. That would remain among my most grievous concerns. A year hence, when I shared this with an elderly, Tibetan Buddhist monk, he asked about the circumstances surrounding Bob's dying and the days after. I told him that Jigme Rinpoche had come to pray within the hour. He grinned. "Your husband is going to be just fine."

To prepare for the afternoon retrieval of the hospital bed, I went into the dining area, the space Bob left behind and began to remove the linens, dropping blanket, pillowcases and sheets onto the floor. I folded the patchwork quilt my grandmother had made for me as a wedding gift. Something she'd been planning since I was born and for which she saved fabric from every dress of my childhood. The night before my wedding, she'd sat down next to me and took it into her lap, turning it over to reveal and point out the minute stitches, "I sewed every patch with these old, arthritic hand and every one with love."

Top sheet, bottom sheet, mattress pad. Gabriel gathered it all into a pile between his front paws, heaved a great sigh and placed his head on top of them. I lay down on the floor and wrapped an arm around him. "I'm sorry." He stared into my eyes. He was fifteen, near the end of his expected life span. "I need you to stick around for this year," I told him. "Then you can do whatever you want."

Memorial Service

THE ALL SOULS CHURCH CARILLON rang seven times and the choir descended from its loft to form a semi-circle around the pews. I'd wanted us to feel embraced as they sang Palestrina's "Tu Es Petrus," one of Bob's and my favorites. I'd had several meetings over the week with Walter Klauss, the much-admired choirmaster and friend. He agreed to my musical requests based on those Bob and I had discussed in a brief interlude near the end when he felt called to speak of "after."

At Rebecca's behest before leaving the apartment, I changed my black dress for a red one. "No black, Mom. So much during these past months has been about joy." She was right as she was about many things. I relied on and trusted her good instincts. Both then and now.

Dear friends, Senior Minister Forrest Church, and Mark Anschutz, former Rector at St. James who'd flown in from Texas, welcomed those who filled the pews. The two men had prayed with Bob whose only religious training had been as a child attending mass with his Catholic nannies. He was moved by daily visits from Forrest and calls from Mark. He had a quarrel with aspects of organized religion, commenting when he accompanied me to a St. James service, "Those people have no idea what they're saying," referring to the recitation of the Nicene Creed. In spite of this, he'd developed a deep and life long spirituality that inspired his intense connection to music, poetry, his constant wonder at our love, and compassion for his patients. He didn't dismiss moments that I considered "miracles," nor the stories I'd heard while on tour for my book about Bobby's death. The many reported, inexplicable "visitations." He was at ease with mystery, knowing when to search for answers and when to let go of the need to know.

When one summer, an assistant rector at St. James asked me to visit a monk in Cambridge who was dying of AIDS, Bob would leave the boat and drive the two hours to accompany me. Before we stepped across the threshold, we sensed the presence of peace that permeated the patient's room. It was clear that he was not alone even when nobody was there.

Our internist once told me, "Bob is the best diagnostician in town." He was a sharp scientist but didn't discount the mysteries of life. Some things, he said, belong to mystery. Unlike many physicians, he didn't believe reality was limited to what could be proven in the lab. Perhaps it gave him the courage with which he faced death. Years ago, at Mark's request Bob had given a Lenten talk about prayer to the parishioners. He believed in its power. He told them, "When you pray, you're not alone." Once, long before cancer I asked him what he prayed for? "To be brave."

Gabriel, wearing one of Bob's floral bow ties in place of a collar lay on the floor next to Rebecca. The box of ashes sat upstairs next to the organ. I'd wrapped it in gold paper and affixed star, moon, and musical note stickers. He loved this organ and Wally, who made it sing. That passion drew him here every Sunday. With music's capacity to bypass the reasoning brain, to go straight and deep into the heart, he was moved to tears. And every Sunday, the music made him weep.

Which is precisely why this was a service of music, something Bob and I had determined years ago and revisited following the diagnosis. "Lots of music," he'd said. "Not a lot of chatter." And so I'd instructed Forrest and Mark to speak very little. "Let the music speak."

Noticing Carol four rows behind us, I motioned for her to sit in the family pew. Bob had always said that love was inclusive, not exclusive. "Love begets more love." She had loved him once long ago. She had raised these magnificent children. That was to be honored.

In the few minutes I'd allotted them, Forrest talked about Bob's "huge capacity for love. He didn't always get it right but when he didn't, he tried again."

Mark spoke of their intense friendship, a bond formed around sailing and spirituality. "What we had most in common was our love for our wives. Boy, do we love our wives." Present tense.

The choir back upstairs sang Maurice Durufle's Ubi Caritas. The music lifted me onto its back and carried me far from death and pain.

"Where true love and charity are found,
God is always there...
Let us all rejoice and be glad, now and always...
And with sincere heart let us love each other now."

I did rejoice and was sated with love. The joy would not last, but I didn't know that. I rested in the knowledge that we had done right by Bob, that he left us on the outgoing tide of our love. As he aged he became more certain of what he'd always believed, that love was all that mattered. That it was the purpose and meaning of our existence, both coming in and going out. It was what attracted him to Christianity, what he believed to be the heart of Christ's message before human beings institutionalized and used it to their own ends, greed, war, orthodoxies. He forgave those who'd wronged him but it wasn't forgiveness as I'd imagined it. In changing from animosity to love, the effect was as if past wrongs were in past and the past was dead. None of this was self-conscious. He did not set out on this path. It was what he became.

Which didn't mean, as I'd warned him in the hospital that he wasn't also capable of being "an asshole." He'd been impatient with one of his private duty nurses, reprimanding her so sharply that when she left the room, I told him, "Until you can start treating these people kindly and with respect, I'm giving you a time out. I'm leaving and not coming back for twenty-four hours." And I did.

When I'd been back at the apartment for an hour, he called and said with great sorrow, "I'm sorry." I was having none of it. "I saw young men who hadn't had a chance to live their full lives dying with more dignity than you." My voice was shaking with rage. Yes, that cliché exists for a reason, because it's the most apt description of what happens when our body joins our mind in its response to passion. Yes, I actually said that to my dying husband. And for good measure, "I expect better of you. I'll see you tomorrow." I hung up before he could say more. There's something about slamming down a phone that is the satisfactory close of such a conversation, the spending of the last bit of fury. What does one substitute with a cell phone?

Months later, I told Rebecca, "I wish I hadn't given him that time out. That wasn't the right thing to do."

"Yes, it was, Mom. He was being an asshole."

I'd always admired her honest responses. When she was in her 20's I told a friend who'd asked after her, "There's something pure about her. Like a brook. She's clear." Which wasn't to say she wasn't fierce. That she couldn't, as she would say, "Lose her shit." Our last Christmas Eve together she forced Bob to "get off your ass," and join us at the table. He tried to explain, "I don't think you understand how sick I am." She didn't, none of us did because he'd been so stoic. But hearing it didn't cause her to relent. He came to the table. He did his best.

The memorial service program had on its cover a photograph of a jubilant Bob at the wheel of Sea Hound. Below it was Whitman's poem from *Leaves of Grass*,

"Now finale to the shore...
Depart upon thy endless cruise, old Sailor!"

As Wally struck up the recessional, I motioned to Rebecca to pick up Gabriel's leash and walk down the aisle. She gave me a you've-got-to-be-kidding look. A he's-your-dog look. She'd never been keen on this replacement for her late Golden Retriever. Gabriel was a one-woman dog. "Twelve years of foreplay and he'll be your friend," I once explained to someone who took offense at his reserve. I gave her the long practiced, "Do it!" look. And so she did, heading down the aisle to the exalting strains of Louis Vierne's Carillon. I felt as exuberant as a bride.

Home After the Service

BACK HOME ALONE as I sat in the hand holding chair, I sensed a light filled, pulsating energy streaming down into my body. I remained transfixed, opening my palms to better receive whatever gift this was. There was no doubting it was a gift. Because it showed no sign of stopping, I wanted to stay like this all night, but there would be a long drive the next day.

Nothing gold can stay.

Ascher, Ashes All Fall Down

THE CHILDREN, Carol, Tshering and I rose early to drive to Woods Hole and the ferry to Martha's Vineyard, Bob's heart's home. It was a cold and gray day into which everything unfolded in a blur. Gone was the vivid translucence of last night.

Once on board, I hesitated to go to the railing. Catching the sea scent of home and sailing might undo me but, within minutes of Bob's death I'd taken a vow, "Say 'yes' to everything." This was the first of my "everything." I leaned out over the water and inhaled deeply as we'd done for thirty-five years. And I was fine...the beginning of no predicting.

Each of us was silent, held within our own rembrance of this ride across the Sound from the mainland to an island imprinted with memories dating from childhood. Perhaps no home ever holds the poignancy and potential heart break as the places that sheltered us as we grew, when we were open to life and wonder and it was all new.

When we arrived at Menemsha Beach, Rebecca noted, "This was his favorite view both going and coming." I was taken aback to find Islanders there to greet us with champagne, strawberries, and chocolate. How did they know we were coming? They just did. Islands are like that.

Carol asked if her husband Bob Hulsizer, who was at their house in Chilmark three miles away could join us on the beach? Of course.

"What the fuck is this?" exclaimed Lynn Murphy, legendary curser, boat mechanic and lifelong Vinyarder. Bob admired Lynn's ability to utter profanities in uninterrupted paragraphs. He called it "poetry" and tried to follow Lynn's example until I put a stop to it when I heard twelve-year-old Steve swear at someone who'd bumped into his dingy. Lynn pointed across the Sound toward the Elizabeth Islands at an improbably garish sunset appearing out of the gloom. "It's been an awful day. Wind, rain. And now this…" He stared out at the flash of magenta, red and orange hues spreading across the sky.

Had we never seen a sunset as dramatic or did the circumstances make it seem so? We'd entered a realm where things occurred and didn't answer to reason.

I hugged him and his wife Susan, the Chilmark postmistress. Rebecca fell into Margaret Maida's arms as she had through many an adolescent turmoil. Margaret was an Up Island heroine descended from generations of islanders thus making her a "real" islander. Following the birth of her fifth child and the realization that her husband, the town cop, was a crook, she divorced him becoming a single mother with no means of support other than waitressing and scalloping in the fall with Lynn — cold, brutal work with a hot-tempered man. Now she was the manager of the local bank. She had offered to feed and house us and we'd accepted.

After greetings, I knelt on the beach and with my index finger drew a catboat in the sand. I put Bob's owner's pennant at the top of the mast and the box of ashes at the helm and then a rogue wave of grief knocked me down and left me gasping for air. Bob Hulsizer approached, helped me up and with his arm around me walked to the water's edge where he pointed toward the fading flare of sunset and said, "There." He too, began to cry.

We returned to join the others who, holding hands, had formed a circle around the sand etched boat and the box incongruously small for the remains of a larger-than-life man. Offshore the bell buoy rang Bob's nautical Bach. Steven read Stanley Kunitz' "The Long Boat."

"When his boat snapped loose
from its mooring...
he tried at first to wave
to his dear ones on shore but...
they had already lost their faces."
At Ellen's behest we sang a traditional Scottish folksong I used
to sing as a lullaby to Rebecca.
"The water is wide, I can't cross o'er
Nor have I wings with which to fly
Bring me a boat that will carry two
And we shall row, my love and I."

As the moon rose behind us and the sun flashed its fireworks
finale, we threw the ashes to the wind, into the blazing red and gold
light, into the water and the sea grasses and across the sand. We
toasted Captain Bob and left two candles burning on the beach. A
green one on the left, a red one on the right. "Red Right Return."

Swans

CHUCK WAS THE ONLY PERSON UP when I came into the kitchen the next morning. He offered to come with me to walk Gabriel on Squibnocket, the ocean beach. We walked in silence. Vulnerable, open and torn in two.

I told him, "When you reenter your life, people will respond as though you've lost a father-in-law, but he was so much more than that, he was like a father to you."

"He was my father."

Suddenly, as though out of nowhere two swans flew over our heads. I'd never seen swans in flight, an experience Bob had been eager for me to share. The beauty of their early evening return to Chilmark Pond had moved him when their undulations moved the air between sea and sky. But I always seemed to have been doing something else, looking at something else, being somewhere else at that hour. This pair above us was dramatic and startling, so white against the about-to-snow, gray sky. We watched as they disappeared beyond the visible stretch of beach. And then they returned, circled above us and flew back the way they had come.

"They mate for life," I said. "Swans do."

I knew in the way that one "knows" before reason comes in to chatter and confuse, I knew that what occurred had been no coincidence. Some things belong to mystery.

Wind

BACK HOME IN NEW YORK, I opened our apartment door to a yawning silence. This was not the seductive, winter silence I'd once experienced while on assignment in Lapland. That silence hummed with what I imagined was Kepler's music of the spheres. No, this was flat, dead, unresponsive.

And then, the wind. Now that we'd exhausted the rituals that confine chaos — the unofficial wake, memorial service and the scattering of the ashes, once I was alone a wind began to blow through the emptiness of my hollowed self. It didn't stop for days and as it rose up my spine and keened in my ears, I began to imagine that this was what Saturn's solar winds sounded like. Or the wind that would rise up if one could hang over the edge of the earth and into the void.

Agony was not unexpected. There were steps I could take to ease and eventually claw my way out of it. For ages, widows had been doing that, their stories in literature, oral traditions and paintings record their pain and release from pain. My situation wasn't singular, only its expression was at times particular as it is for everyone who has lost a beloved. But this was nothing I'd read or heard about, this physical response to the intensity of torment. Grief is experienced in hyperbole. When the wind continued for days, I began to understand why Lear went mad.

Over dinner at a small bistro on the west side where a friend, another recent widow and I often dined to reassure each other we weren't alone in this torment, I described what was happening. She put down her fork and looked at me. "Yes, I'm having that. That wind inside, but I wasn't going to tell anyone. They'd think I was losing my mind." She couldn't afford to lose her mind. She had to take it to work every day. No one must know.

Agreed.

You'll Think You're Sane

"YOU'LL THINK YOU'RE SANE, but you're not," a neighbor called out to me as we crossed the avenue in opposite directions.

She lived in my building. She'd heard the news. We'd shared elevators across the years as our children grew and left us. We knew each other's first names. In Manhattan, that's considered intimacy. Intimate enough to offer advice and opinions. Her husband died five years ago giving her standing to issue such proclamations.

"During the first year," she called over her shoulder before disappearing into our neighborhood deli.

Nonsense, I thought. My husband died two weeks ago and look! I'm doing pretty well, albeit with a wind roaring within. I'm dressed. I made my bed. I'm on the street upright and putting one foot in front of the other.

I shared the certainty of all mad people that I was perfectly sane. I wouldn't think otherwise even months later. As I walked to my hotel after a day teaching a writing workshop sponsored by the University of Chicago, I turned to follow a thin, long legged man wearing a tweed sports jacket and carrying a book under his arm. I wanted to catch up and ask, "Will you marry me?" Lucky for both of us that he was a fast walker and a Chicago chill slapped me back to my senses.

"You'll always be attracted to that body type," a social worker was to tell me. Funny because two serious relationships after Bob's death would be with a fat man and a teeny, tiny, bird-boned man only three inches taller than my 5'2." I could wear his socks.

I was "perfectly sane" the first Christmas season following Bob's death when looking at lipsticks at C.V.S., I heard Andy Williams' voice singing over the store speakers, "I'll be home for Christmas." I gasped and raced to a salesclerk, "I've got to speak to the manager! Where is the manager?" She rushed ahead of me and when we found him, I begged, "Turn this off! Please turn the music off!" Alarmed, he wrung his hands against his helplessness. "I don't know how!"

Nor would I question my sanity when that summer on assignment for the Times Travel Magazine, I decided to kayak rather than raft down the Middle Fork of the Salmon River's notorious white waters. Because I'd never been in a kayak and was incapable of navigating a whirlpool, the boat flipped and the current sucked me down, down, down. As I was drowning, I thought, "Rebecca is going to kill me." But the river burped. As I surfaced and clung to a rock, the pale guide muttered, "Thought I was gonna lose that one."

I would see nothing insane about lusting after beach boys in Cuba where Jim and Kevin Abernathy had taken me within two weeks of Bob's death. All details taken care of, all expenses paid. How brave of them to be alone with one so raw with grief.

They knew nothing of my attraction to Cuban men who had a reputation for poetic, passionate lovemaking. I was missing that. Then I recalled Rebecca's warning upon my departure, "Don't you dare come home with an STD", so I went to a museum instead.

I would not think my response was crazed when our homebound flight tumbled and bucked and I thought, "I don't care. Go ahead and crash." I would fail to consider that the other passengers might care a lot.

Oh, yes. In that first year I would be insane and the self-absorption — an unfortunate characteristic of grief — would suck me down as the river did.

When the editor of my first two books, a widow and my most stoic and reserved acquaintance warned, "Expect six bad years,"

I thought, "Loser. I don't have time for that." I would learn that she chose that number because she hadn't yet lived through the seventh, eighth, or ninth. She hadn't been slammed by the tenth anniversary.

When I met her on the street that many years later I said, "More like ten years."

"At least," said she before moving on.

But I knew none of that the day my neighbor predicted madness. No. I thought, you might be crazy, but not I.

Reaching Across the Void

ON THE RARE OCCASION when able to sleep, I dreamed that Bob was alive. When I awakened in this cold bed and reached for his warmth there was nothing but the shock of emptiness. The shock and surprise of his absence again and again and again.

Morning is among grief's cruelties because sleep swallows reality and then releases you to the news. You have to do this again and again before it's no longer a surprise. No longer news. This morning I said aloud, "Fuck this!" And got out of bed. I preferred not to sleep.

Dora Carrington dreaded mornings following the death of her long-time companion, writer and critic Lytton Strachey. She wrote in her diary, "I dreamt of you again last night. And when I woke up it was as if you had died afresh." She withstood two months of such mornings before borrowing a friend's gun and putting an end to them.

Although not suicidal I understood her response. In fact, Montaigne appears to have found such an outcome desirable. In his essay, *Three Good Women*, he lauds those who act on the phrase, "I can't live without you."

He cites Arria, wife of Paetus who plunged her husband's dagger into her breast to encourage her husband, Paetus, to do likewise after his imprisonment by the Emperor Claudius. Placing the bloodied instrument in his hand, she said, ''Believe me, the wound that I have made does not pain me, but the wound that you are to give yourself, that O Paetus, pains me." Such a good woman.

Pliny the Younger had a neighbor whose wife persuaded him

that only death would rid him of the pain of his disease (which I believe may have been no more than a bladder infection, but such a detail would have offended Montaigne's sensibilities.) She promised to accompany him as they leapt from their window into the sea. "But for fear that the closeness of her embrace might be loosened by the fall and by terror, she had herself tightly bound and attached to him around the waist."

Only in the case of Paulina, wife of Seneca, did attempted suicide fail. Not to worry, says Montaigne. Such failure did not diminish her honor, virtue and devotion, "showing by the pallor of her face how much of life had flowed away through her wounds."

Because we've come such a long way as women, it would hurt my pride to follow the examples of these "good" women. Although anquished, I had reason to live. Even though I felt as though every cell in my body were screaming for him. My skin missed his skin. Without it, my own was never warm. My lips, my eyelids mourned the loss of his lips. My fingers carried the memory of his shoulder blades. My cheeks the memory of his cheeks. My body yearned like a prayer into the absence.

No, I would not kill myself, but given the choice of being banished to the streets, to wander this city for the rest of my life in exchange for one more night holding him in my arms... Lead me to him!

Fear of Bathing

FEAR OF BATHING.
Fear of music.
Fear of salt water.
Fear of the video store.
Fear of Saturday nights.
Fear of rainy nights.
Fear of decision-making.
Fear of change.

All perfectly reasonable, I thought. When Bob was alive, I took nightly, long, luxurious baths with a book in hand. Now, to do so would be perilous. I'd be unable to escape in time. Escape from what? I couldn't tell you. An intruder. The ultimate intruder had already been through here.

I also feared that in my nakedness I'd be cold in the bath, no matter the heat of the water. Since Bob's death, I was always sucking warmth in layers of turtleneck shirts and sweaters by day, long underwear, flannel pajamas and wool socks at night.

I limited water in the tub to about three inches, hopped in and remained standing as I scrubbed with soap before lying down to rinse. Very quickly. So cold. When I emerged, the air stung my wet skin.

Fear of music. It would break my heart.
Fear of salt water. It would break my heart.
Fear of the video store. It would break my heart.
Fear of our favorite restaurant. It would break my heart.
Our summers in and on salt water.

Cozy, sexy, rainy nights.

Saturday afternoons spent in passion.

Saturday nights, dining at the bar of our favorite neighborhood bistro, then home to bed and an old movie from the video store, my head on his chest.

Then came terror — fear with sharp fingernails.

I was in a state of terror when engaged in the ordinary walk home from the library's writers' room.

Terrified when a motorcycle passed.

Terrified of losing my keys.

Terrified that an acquaintance might stop for a sidewalk chat.

Terrified of the bald woman walking east on 84th Street.

On occasion rage arose to act as a shield against the terror. I was enraged by the sight of that man sitting in his top down, blue Corvette. He'd lived in this neighborhood as long as I had. He'd taken to backcombing his shaggy hair and thinking we were all still in Woodstock and groovy. His shorts were too tight and too short. As I passed him, I thought, "You are ridiculous!"

Well, he was.

Mourning begins as an amorphous, unrelenting anxiety that hovers somewhere just south of the heart and north of the gut. It began when we heard the diagnosis. It stole our appetites, our ability to sleep. Now it flared into fear, terror and this. James Dao reported in the Times that more than five percent of dogs used by Marines "to track Taliban fighters and bomb makers" and those that accompany SEALS on secret missions were developing Post Traumatic Stress disorders.

"Some become hyper-vigilant. Others avoid buildings or work areas that they had previously been comfortable in."

I rest my case.

"You'll think you're sane but, you're not."

Darkness Impenetrable

DESPAIR MOVED IN and began rearranging the physical and psychic furniture. My cheeks were sunken, my body near skeletal. I could not read. It took a long time before I could piece together the words forming the New York Time's headlines. I could no longer tolerate poignancy. It didn't surprise me to learn that harpist and music patron Yoko Ceschina never played the harp again following the death of her husband. Her harps sat untouched in the basement. Who could stand to allow those ethereal sounds to flow through the fingers? Grief abhors beauty.

Things changed on a cellular level. Perhaps you've read the happy news that if several times a week, we exercise vigorously enough to be able to breathe but not speak, it affects cells connected to aging. We can be younger if we don't die on the treadmill. I contend that grief also alters our cells. It ages them. There is no such thing as post-traumatic stress syndrome. There is only stress syndrome. Yes, dogs and drugs can help but they don't change our cell mutations. My former sleep patterns never recovered after my brother's illness and death and that was a long, long time ago.

Someday, they'll do us a favor and scan the brains of those whose beloveds are dying, are dead. A randomized, controlled study from diagnosis to death, following the subjects for a decade postmortem. We need to tell our stories and wouldn't it be fine if pictures of our brains would do the work for us in language bereft of hysteria or cool remove? Pure, irrefutable science for all to see; this is what the brain looks like when the bottom falls away from your world, when you've lost your bearings. This is the brain adapting to survive, the brain of a slimy, primordial creature sprouting legs to slouch into a new world.

Until those scans come along, we should be treated like patients behind the locked doors of a burn unit with its warning sign, "Do Not Enter!" We've been peeled of our protective layers.

Without scans, without warning signs how would anyone who hadn't experienced loss "know how you feel?" Bless those who don't make that claim. Bless those who offer to run errands, make a cup of tea, sit with us and do nothing. It takes courage and equanimity to be quietly present for another's pain. Bless those who don't think something's amiss when "sufficient time" has passed and we're still sad. Unless it's been lived, there is no way of knowing that grief mends in patches. And then rips out the stitches.

No, there is no knowing because as Iris Murdoch claimed, "Bereavement is a darkness impenetrable to the imagination of the unbereaved."

As it must be if the world is to function. We need the "unbereaved" to carry the ball for the rest of us. If they don't put one foot in front of the other, if they don't know it's the Metro card, not the AMEX card that is swiped in the subway turnstile slot, if they don't get out of bed in the morning to carry out the work of the world, what would become of us? Imagine if they knew what we knew? They would be awash in tears. Slosh, slosh, slosh.

How would the "unbereaved" understand the loss of energy? Mine was depleted today by trying to focus as an estate buyer, a crafty obituary reader looked around Bob's office, gave a French sniff of dismissal and said he had no use for the mid-century furniture, but, he'd take it off my hands and even pay the moving costs. Fine, fine. Sure. Back to bed.

It Don't Look the Same

"IT DON'T LOOK THE SAME," A lifelong resident of Joplin, Missouri, told an NPR reporter. It don't look the same since the tornado raged through town ripping leaves, branches, roots from trees and roofs from homes. Her neighbors say they can't find their way around places that were familiar just last night.

It don't look the same here, either. I was lost in space. Death had stormed through and flattened what my eyes and heart once rested upon. I couldn't find my way around the formerly familiar.

I lost things. As though a force of nature blew through town and carried away my glasses, papers, keys, shoes. I left jackets and sweaters on the backs of restaurant chairs. God knows where I left my keys. "Has anybody seen my…" became a familiar refrain.

When I spoke of this to another widow whose storm blew through town three years ago, she said, "Of course you lose things. That's what we do. We've lost everything, so what's the difference?"

What I didn't lose, I started to give away. The unconscious letting go became deliberate. I went into forfeiture frenzy. What was the difference? What were possessions when the possessor was no more?

Here! Here! Does anybody want…? A friend suggested, "Rent a storage unit for Bob's things for awhile before deciding what to keep and what to give away." She was probably right. Maybe I shouldn't have been doing this while the internal wind continued to howl. But I did. I gave most of his tools to Steve and Chuck. His cable chargers to the handyman. I gave his tuxedo to a feckless boy who needed one for his prom. Sure. There it was in its Paul

Stuart box. I threw in the shirt, studs and dancing pumps for good measure. What was I supposed to do? Cast them in bronze as my grandmother did with my baby shoes?

I wanted to burn the bed. No, a friend of Bob's said. "Don't burn the bed. Honor the bed."

After consulting with the children, I shipped Oriental rugs to Ellen and drove to Cambridge with Bob's grandmother's fine linens, the large black and white photo of Sea Hound in a race under full sail with Carol and the three kids on board that had hung in Bob's office. Etchings and oils inherited from their grandfather Charles. I drove downtown to give the nautical library and every volume of the complete works of Freud to Housing Works Thrift Shop and Book Store.

My giving away was a primal, preemptive strike. I was giving away because you can't take what I don't have. I had had Bob and he was taken. As were his starlit nights, green gloamings, sunsets, rising crescent moons. I could not fathom the grief of losing this life with its spring breezes, Orion, the Big Dipper, Cassiopeia, twilight's display. Perhaps I was identifying with the aggressor death, acting out part of its pageant. Perhaps there was something in the pageantry of sacrifice that brought me closer to Bob's experience. Give away as fate had taken away; turn my back on possessions held dear. A bloodletting.

Take this sixty-year-old record collection. I refused to entertain the sentimental, to allow myself to dwell on the record I held in my hand — Rose, Stern and Istomin playing, Brahms Double Concerto, Bob's first gift to me. "The most beautiful love song ever written," according to his accompanying, note. I was so weary of weeping, so weary of missing.

Take the stereo system. Take the sheet music and the piano with its deep, rich mellowing when Rebecca played Chopin, and she and I together played Bach Busoni for Bob on his fiftieth birthday. Yes, take the piano on which Bob fiddled with jazz riffs before dinner, happy, smiling, pleased with himself.

He'd once dreamed of playing in a bar, a dream tucked in among others that would have drawn on his talents. Professional photographer, violinist, obstetrician, pediatrician, around the world sailor.

Naturally, there was to be no future in smoky bars, no long-legged woman perched atop the piano singing, "Stormy Weather." But as I grilled the fish his playing "Don't Get Around Much Anymore" made it so.

I sold the boat. Without telling Bob, I'd called the broker from the hospital, explained the situation and told him to put it on the market, knowing it might take a long time to find the right buyer. Yes, it seemed out of place to be telling a distant acquaintance that Bob would be dead by summer. It was uncharacteristic to do such a thing without discussing it with my husband, but he deserved the space he needed for hope and denial should they come. The dying get to call those shots.

But I had to call the business shots. The best I could do was get through the business of death. Sell the boat, sell the apartment, pay the medical bills, chase down the insurance companies, make decisions about the possessions. What I knew I would not be able to bear was driving to the shipyard in Padanaram, Massachusetts to empty the boat once it was sold. Climbing on board and seeing his methodically furled lines would be a needle to the heart. Those days, that was not a metaphorical consideration. I feared catching the familiar scent of mildew and brine. I knew if I saw the towel Bob wore inside the neck of his foul weather jacket when we sailed in Nor'easters, I would feel as though one had carried me away. Drowned at sea.

There would come a time when I would wish I'd kept the chiming boat clock, the barometer, lines, chains and anchors, wish I'd put them in the storage bin my friend suggested. I could have visited them as one visits a grave. I could have picked up the lines and tied bowlines and double half hitches. I could have held my hand against the cold steel of anchors that held us firm in stormy harbors. I could have seen Bob's elegant hands pulling on its line, testing whether it had set and turning to me at the wheel with smiling satisfaction once it had. I could have remembered how the boat danced at that anchor through the night rocking us like babies in buntings. And I could have remembered awakening to the shouts of other skippers that prompted us to throw on our foul weather gear and run up on deck to fend off approaching vessels whose anchors had dragged as a storm blew through Cuttyhunk Harbor. I could have remembered how the rain felt like bb's shot at our eyes. I could remember how when the shouting was over, we went below, took off our wet gear, shook ourselves like dogs, dried our hair and feet and poured a shot of single malt scotch, neat.

I retrieved none of it and now, nothing was familiar. Even the familiar was unfamiliar as it was for the citizens of Joplin. The difference was that the neighborhood where we lived and worked for some thirty-five years was not upended, not blown to bits. I still had a home. Albeit one that had become a strange, strange place. The cast of light, the edges of buildings were different without Bob passing by moving the air.

"Rent storage."

She was right. Perhaps nothing more profound than that would come from my individual experience. Perhaps this grief had no existential meaning, no lesson, no St. John of the Cross moment of burning life's excesses to ash to reveal the soul. Perhaps the only wisdom gained from a beloved's death was, "rent storage."

And Then I Lose…

BUT YOU CAN'T RENT STORAGE for a language. If that were possible the world wouldn't be losing a language every two weeks and I wouldn't be losing mine.

That was more grievous than losing my glasses, papers, keys, shoes and jackets. Once the words are gone, so go the stories that define us, that remind us who we are, who the other person is and what we're all doing here together. Without the words, how do we talk our way home?

No longer hearing and speaking the language of my tribe, my captain and crew, I feared I was losing the thread that bound us.

Smokey sou'wester
Triangle, sextant and chart
Fly the ensign
Tumble home
Baggy wrinkle
Scuttlebutt
Blue Peter
Old Salt
Hawser
Hull down
Charlie Noble
Soundings
Fid
Ditty bag
Poop deck
Yar

Hogged hull

Spindrift

Boson's chair ("The ensign is fouled. Send Steven up in the boson's chair.")

Flying jenny

Grab the boathook! Pick up the mooring!

Fuck!

Goddamn!

I: "How do you know that boat's a Sparkman and Stephens?"

Bob: "How do you know your own mother?"

Our once vital language had become one of nostalgia calling forth the essence of home, relegated to the language of longing. A torch song.

There's Always the Chance
They Might Come Back

I'D LIVED IN THIS APARTMENT since arriving as a college student with a pack on my back, the size of the one with which I'll leave. Bob knew New York. He made all the arrangements while I had the luxury of being a student in Vermont writing papers on Renaissance poets.

When I arrived to see what was to be our home, it looked just right, less than a block from his office, lots of light and air. A second bedroom for a someday baby. No, none of those "good bones" and limestone of pre-war "integrity." It didn't meet the standards of Paul Goldberger, other architectural critics, and old money. Fine with me. It seemed like a suitable place for happiness. I continued to commute to Bennington and returned to Bob on weekends.

With time the baby came, joining our dinner table regulars — my stepchildren, our friends. I imagined that the walls absorbed those years we cast off like sighs. I sensed that stored within them was all the love, anger, forgiveness, laughter, pronouncements and questions expressed over those years. If I pressed my ear against this one in the dining room, if I demanded of those around me a Raymond Carver silence, "Will you please be quiet, please," I imagined I'd hear the mumblings of time. Half sentences. A Pentecostal chaos of conversations. Hot headed, all night arguments with friends about the war in Vietnam, the Chicago Seven, Nixon, Watergate, the Black Power movement.

"Stop paying taxes. Put them in escrow."

"Move to Canada."

"You what? You're going to help Angela Davis escape?"

Mourning the assassinated. Bobby Kennedy. Martin Luther King.

Baby Rebecca's projectile vomiting after she'd nurse, my otherwise exuberant dinnertime reports to her father, "She's extraordinary. Today she…" Bob's warning her as a teenager, "If you ever do drugs, I'll break your fucking neck." Steve's and Bob's discussions when he came to live with us, taking a year off from college to consider what to do with his life.

"What would you do if you could do anything you wanted, not what you think you 'should' do?"

"Be a filmmaker."

"Then be a filmmaker."

There would be the echo of Lizzie's and Bob's shared passion for medicine. While she was a studying at uptown at Columbia Presbyterian Medical School, Lizzie would use five-year-old Rebecca as her guinea pig. "Lie down, let me palpate your abdomen."

In among all those murmurs would be the inconsequential shared between husband and wives.

"I saw Sam on the street this afternoon…"

"It was a hard day at the office."

"I'm having trouble writing this column due tomorrow. What if I never pull it together?"

"Then borrow my optimism."

Attempts to comfort. Rebecca's crying about the mean girl in her class, "It's no fair! She should be punished!" And Bob's responding, "Her life is her punishment." Solace after my stepdaughter's break ups with boyfriends.

Music of summers past played in the winter to remind Lizzie, Ellen and me of the abandon with which we sang along with the radio when I was driving us up or down island. "Come on baby, light my fire…" Dancing within the confines of our seat belts, pounding out the beat on the steering wheel. "Come and set the night on fiiiiiiirrrre."

There would be a constant staccato of Bob's reaction to everything I put before him at dinner. "Beautiful." Sometimes he didn't even look up from his book, saying it before seeing what I served. It didn't matter. It was the appreciation that mattered and he never failed at that. It was to be a cold, cold absence when I started cooking for other men. Like stepping outside into a January night. Freezing silence.

I believed the walls of my new home would be bereft of family history. I had no choice but to leave this place. I couldn't afford to hold onto real estate for a ghost. When the contract for sale had been signed and I called Rebecca to tell her, I burst into tears, acting out Blaise Pascal's assertion, "...we dream of times that are not and blindly flee the only one that is. The fact is that the present usually hurts."

"What's the matter, Mom? This is good news."

"If he comes back, where will he go?"

And there you have it. It takes a long time, a really long time to stop believing that they just might walk through that door.

Yes, it was good news. Good news that I would no longer be paying maintenance and mortgage interest on both Bob's office and our apartment. Good news that Bob's office was in a 700 square feet, one-bedroom apartment on the eleventh floor of a residential building, good thing that I knew how to remodel a confined space as though I were building a boat. A boat floating above the East River, "sailing to Queens," Steve noted from the terrace.

But what if he came back? He would want to return to his practice in this spot, to this chair looking out at the river that steadied him. He was not one whose feet were completely at home on terra firma. He was most himself, most comfortable in his own skin when at the helm beneath a full sail. He felt "grounded" only after casting off. Yes, this is where he would want to be. What if he came to our old apartment and found strangers there? I didn't want him to be confused, to panic.

I'd been trying to sell the office for a year, but the co-op board turned down each potential buyer. Boards have leeway for caprice and it's practiced most by those for whom this is their only power. They make the decision who's in, who's out and owe no explanation. It was only when I ran into a member of the Board as I was walking the dog that I got an answer I insisted upon. She told me that those who wanted to buy were either too rich (they'd use it as a pied-a-terre, "this isn't a hotel, you know,") or not rich enough to meet the building's financial requirements. Or so she'd said.

Not long after, the solution came to me as I was returning from teaching at Bennington. As I drove down the Molly Stark Byway, a winding, two lane road, the scenic route home, up, up, up to the top of Hogback Mountain where we skied as children, and then down, down, down following the curves to the other side. Just like skiing. It was then while I was thinking about not much that I "heard" Bob say, "When something doesn't work again and again, stop bumping into the same wall. Turn around and go in a different direction." With that, I knew the precise direction. Our apartment building's co-op board was more amenable. Members were our friends aware of the situation. When I got home, I let them know I was going to sell and would appreciate a speedy approval, which there was.

And now I worried he'd come back and not find me there.

I didn't know that this move would take me to a place that would become my safe haven, where there was room for only one and I would rejoice in that.

Once when sailing alone after taking a friend to the mainland, Bob had been socked in by fog and found his way home by smell alone. I'd stayed behind with our 8-month-old daughter. Fear mounted as fog thickened and night fell and I began to imagine our infant as fatherless and I a widow. Lost at Sea was something you saw on a lot of tombstones in the cemeteries of these islands.

Had I not been frantic, I would have rested in the knowledge that Bob was never lost when afloat. He had an internal compass. He knew every rock and shoal and schedule of tides on these waters between Noman's Land and Martha's Vineyard.

And yet, he should have sailed into the harbor hours ago. I thought of the long cables that stretched between tugs and barges. More than one fog bound sailor had sailed directly into the steel towline between them. Mast down, man decapitated. The tug captain unaware would continue on his way like the boat that sailed on as Icarus fell from the sky.

I resisted calling the Coast Guard because I didn't want to diminish Bob's pride in his seamanship. Those were the days before cell phones and satellite navigation. When one was afloat, news was sent and received over ship to shore radios. Anyone could listen. There would be talk. I gave Bob more time to find his own way.

And he did. The moment I'd decided to place the call. When he walked in the door, the fog still thick on his eyelashes, his foul weather jacket slick, he said, "I smelled the blueberry bushes on Noman's Land and knew where I was. From there I just ghosted along."

There are so many near misses in life. Sometimes, they revisit at 3 a.m. flashbacks. Often riding that tide of the dark hour is the memory of my younger sister who when heading home to Cuttyhunk from a picnic at Quicks Hole became disoriented in the fog and missed the entrance to the harbor. Sailing past the island and headed out to sea, she followed the sound of the Texas Tower's foghorn, knowing that other boats would navigate by that and if she was lucky, would see her. And so, one did. A sloop responded to her flashlight's s.o.s signal and with its radar, lead her home into the harbor. By that time, islanders were distressed. She was four hours overdue — time enough for the grownups to imagine the worst. And then, there she was.

And here was my husband long-striding across the porch and through the screen door. Smiling.

You see, it can happen. They can disappear and emerge from the fog.

Think about the missing climber on Everest, presumed dead. Until another group of climbers stumbled upon him. "He was just sitting there." They didn't know nor could they imagine how he'd survived. But he had. It can happen.

Consider Hiroo Onondo, a Japanese intelligence officer in WW II who was discovered in 1974 hiding in the mountains of Lubong Island in the Philippines. He didn't know the war was over. The jig was up.

Consider Ulysses. Penelope didn't know if she would be weaving for the rest of her days. It was possible. But he returned, his dog greeted him, and Athena held back the dawn.

It could happen. Bob could walk out of the fog and return to me. Of course, he wouldn't. But let's just say for argument's sake, should he return and take me into his arms, I wouldn't let go. I'd watch him like a hawk.

This time if he got lost, I'd find him by the scent of his skin. My island in the fog. My home. I'd find him by scent alone.

But he was not coming back. Ever.

I was twice stunned. Once more I was struck by the blow of this awareness and the realization that I still held onto the possibility of his walking through the door.

I would hold my heart open and ready for him to move back in.

I was changing my address, but I was not going to have a change of heart.

The Wrong Parent Died

SHE STOPPED JUST SHORT OF SAYING SO.

Our team of two bound for three months by common struggle disbanded. We were a splintered girl group. Martha and the Vandellas. The Spice Girls. The Supremes. There was discord among members of Death and Dying. We were off key, unable to find the harmonic chord. She predicted this the night of Bob's death as we held each other celebrating that we'd accomplished what we'd set out to do. She had said, "And now we'll be on separate paths. Each of us to grieve in our own way."

I had no idea how much pain would come from those diverging paths. Taking care of Bob had been teamwork. Now that it was over, I feared that our tight bond of a lifetime would unravel. How could I know that in a short period of time we would resume our devotion to one another? That our paths would merge again? That we would once more be a team? That we would seek each other out and find joy in the company? Grief makes it impossible to imagine a better future.

I wasn't surprised by her bursts of anger. "Stop trying to grieve the 'right' way," she said referring to my public stoicism. I'd had the experience that when someone dies, the target of inevitable rage is the person you could trust to not stop loving you. I knew had I died first, Bob would have been the "wrong one." The survivor can only be who she's always been and can't become the missing person as well. But this was reason and reason is no foil for torment. You might as well hold up a feather as a shield against a hurricane.

Rebecca had drawn ever closer to Bob when she was seven and

I entered law school. He became the parent in charge. She could call him on the intercom that connected home to office. She'd walk around the corner to visit when he called to say the last patient had left. She accompanied him on spring weekends to sand, varnish and paint the boat and once finished, sail it. They were bound in their shared misery that I'd "abandoned" (her words at the time) them for case law. For Marbury v. Madison

They comforted each other with rituals. Tonight, at dinner I failed to practice one. I didn't pick up the cue when she put her palm down on the table. She pointed to it. "Oh. Right." I put mine on top of hers but didn't repeat the motion when she put hers on top of mine. Her eyes filled with tears. "You can't even do that right." She was joking but, not really. I didn't know how to make the "love sandwich" she shared with Bob when they dined together. Hand upon hand upon hand upon hand.

Nothing could make his absence "right." I lacked his wisdom. His clarity. His fearless ability to tell it as it was, how he saw it. Bob had the capacity to acknowledge and right wrongs caused by his temper. In Rebecca's date book is a note emblematic of that.

Dated July 15, 1998, when she was thirty years old: "Dear Rebec: Thank you deeply for the lovely note. I'd plead the same as you: I'm wise…when I am, and m'shugina when I'm that. So, the people who love us steer in between, and correct our course when we're lost in the fog. Much love always Dad."

There you had it. Open, honest, vulnerable and forgiving. That was their relationship. And always "Much love."

I agreed with her. The wrong parent had died.

But Then

BUT THREE MONTHS LATER, she said, "What you need, Mom is a bit of Paris." And in a reversal of old roles, she invited me to be her guest on a writing assignment. Those were the glory days when journals were flush.

I hesitated. Did I want to be alone with someone so easily angered by me? Then reminded myself of my deathbed vow that in the first year I would say, "Yes" to everything and so I did.

After college, she'd entered what I referred to as "the family biz," becoming a writer first at People Magazine followed by Entertainment Weekly for which she was reporting on The Cannes Film Festival with a stop-off in Paris. I was to tag along until she went on to Cannes. I had enough miles for a round trip ticket. It would cost me nothing. So, yes, yes.

Once there, we shared a room and a featherbed. We feasted on morning croissants, afternoon saucissons, twilight macrons, and late-night wines. We wandered without maps or plans. "This street looks promising…"

As we strolled through the Tuileries garden, I said something that made her respond with, "Mom, you are certifiably insane," and we burst into gales of laughter as powerful as keening complete with its tears and howls. When it subsided, we stared at each other. "Wow," we said in unison. "That felt good."

And that lit a fire beneath my feet., strengthened my resolve to put distance between myself and the place where the pain resided, far from home — that haunt of cold, throbbing absence, where no footsteps approached, no one stirred the air.

I'd travel light and fast. Once home, I called my long time editors at the New York Times and National Geographic Traveler pitching articles that would take me far, far away. I was holding out hope for a cure any place but here. Hoping for back-to-back assignments, meeting deadlines, keeping busy and focused. Yes. Sure. San Diego which would allow a visit with Ellen. A ranch in Wyoming, great I could take Lizzie who loved to ride. Idaho, a landscape large enough to absorb my sorrow. Ireland. A 2,000 mile, solo road trip through Appalachia.

I'd been fortunate in my Times editor, Nancy Newhouse. We'd worked together since the early '80s when having given up the law to return to writing I wrote the Hers column about love and other follies. Infidelity, homelessness, men's clubs, Jean Harris. When Nancy moved to the "Travel" section, I went along. "Wherever you go, that's where I'm going. Even if its Popular Mechanics."

But before all that, I visited the children in Cambridge two more times, returned to San Diego and Ellen. I was determined to keep our connection, to let them know as they had let me, that they were mine forever.

Grief and love are stubborn. As I traveled far from home, they refused to stay behind; they cling, feeding upon themselves, they can trick you into thinking that nothing has changed.

Two months after Bob's death, when I'd arrived at a destination, I reached for the old-fashion landline to place the habitual call. "Hello. I'm here. I miss you. I love you." I stared in disbelief at my hand holding the receiver as the dial tone droned.

I'd reasoned grief couldn't keep up with a jet plane, wouldn't find me if I left no forwarding address, no song lines.

"You'll think you're sane but, you're not."

And yet, I tried because it's in the tradition to travel to mend a broken heart.

Young women in unsuitable matches were sent on the grand tour by well-meaning 19th-century parents. In the wake of his wife, Clover's suicide, Henry Adams headed for Chartres and Mont-St.-Michel. I've known women who as dutiful wives had stayed close to home but once widowed, set out for the far reaches of the earth. It puts grief in context when you stand on the ruins of ancient civilizations and realize that suffering has always been the human condition. Spouses and lovers have been ripped from one another since the beginning of time. You need only look at the two young lovers embracing atop a carved marble Etruscan tomb, wander through the Roman Forum and pause before the ruins of the Temple of the Vestal Virgins to put loss in perspective. Imagine little girls taken from home and parents in order to be trained to guard the flame. Should one of them slumber or daydream and allow the flame to die, she was buried alive.

Context, context is the mourner's equivalent of the real estate agent's "location, location." I would learn that it was easier to get out of bed in the morning if I imagined being in the company of every woman who had lost a beloved. The tens of thousands of widows of the Khmer Rouge, widows of 9/11, widows of the mean streets, widows of tires skidding on slick, wet pavement, Cherokee widows of the Trail of Tears, widows of lynchings, police brutality, poverty and inequity, of the Peloponnesian Wars, widows of Congo. Little did I know that within a few years this sisterhood would include hundreds of thousands whose spouses would be victims of a virus determined to take us out. With my eyes closed, I would visualize gathering these multitudes into my arms and I would say aloud, "O.K. Let's be brave, let's get up and start the day."

For a time, I stepped out of myself and into these other lives. My own pain diminished in a chorus of ancient suffering. There was a subtle loosening of the chimera's grip on my heart.

As it was when I was on assignment far from home. But a journey is defined by leave-taking and homecoming. What is home without the embrace at both?

What is homecoming without Penelope and a dog? What was homecoming without Bob sitting in his chair reading as I came through the door, then rising to hold and follow me into the bedroom as I unpacked and recounted tales of my wanderings?

Now, when I opened the door of home it was as though I were stepping into a wilderness. No Bob in his reading chair. No Bob anywhere. The first time, it knocked me to my knees before I'd even closed the door behind me.

Driving home alone through driving rain after a visit to Lizzie and Steve in Cambridge, I longed for the person who should have been beside me, sharing a summary of the trip, "The kids were in great shape, don't you think?" Like that. Maybe he'd be waiting when I came through the door.

No. Of course not.

I went into Bob's closet, and buried my head in his shirts, hoping to sniff out any lingering scent. I looked down and saw the dog doing the same, his nose in a long dressing gown. And then I heard the sound of an animal in agony, before realizing it was coming from me.

In Bruges there is a large, vibrant painting of a saint being flayed alive. Upon entering the gallery where it hangs, I became lightheaded and had to sit on the floor with my head between my knees. A guard approached and asked if I were o.k. I shook my head and pointed to the painting, "Does this happen often? Do people faint when they see it?" He thought before recalling, "There was a Girl Scout once..."

In the early years of grief, that painting hung from a hook in my heart.

When people assured, "There will be a time when you'll just have happy memories." I didn't ask, "What do you mean by 'happy?'" "What do you mean by time?" Nobody knows the meaning of time.

He Inhabited Every Season

I LIVED THROUGH EACH and he inhabited every season as the haunt of July jubilation, Christmas joys, pervasive gratitude at the end of the calendar year. Seasons held the same poignancy as smell, taste, music. These were the things that brought not just memory but the griefs and joys they carried. Seasons can cause us to slip out of the grasp of the here and now, of reason and control.

In summer, I could still sense the sticky, cold slick of the fore-deck beneath my bare feet, the soft cashmere of his blue sweater as he sat in the rocking chair on our summer porch.

I could feel and smell the salty sweat of his tennis shirt when in spring he'd return from doubles. My fingers remembered lifting his flannel pajama collar to fight winter nights' chill. Memories are sense sensations, emotional ghost limbs.

The feet the arms, ears, eyes, our entire bodies have stored within them traces of moments we have lived. I echoed Francesca's lament in Dante's *Inferno*. "No grief surpasses this… in the midst of misery to remember bliss."

When spring arrived that first year, I addressed it aloud, "How dare you?" You with your flagrant frippery, frivolity and abandon. Lurid, brazen spring bursts forth no matter the human condition or mood.

Iris Murdoch mused, "People from a planet without flowers would think we must be mad with joy the whole time to have such things about us: white campion, self-heal, bryony, vetch." Well, they'd be wrong.

Self-heal is irony in bloom. White campion, bryony and vetch sharpened their soil-piercing spears when the snow melted, the air softened, birds called, sticky green leaves sprouted, boys swaggered and girls bared their midriffs.

Spring strutted and I stood on the sidelines, the widows' designated place if she didn't struggle to be part of the game.

I tried to throw myself into the maelstrom of living and breathing, conversing and loving and yet, every once in awhile, out of nowhere came the arm of the coach, pulling me out of the game. I just didn't have what it took.

Days like this made me want to take to my bed. The only problem was that upon awakening, I'd be no place better than my bed.

I experienced anticipatory dread. We were heading closer to the season of wind, heat, and sailing. Bob's season.

With the sweep and rush of April winds, with rain washing winter from the city, his spirits would lift. He'd hold his head to the air like a dog alert to a scent. Tennis! Sailing! "You, you, you," he would say to me.

Once the children were grown and no longer cruising with us, he said as we drove alone with the dog to Padanaram to load and launch the boat, "One of the things I love about the boat is I have you all to myself." I didn't say, "One of the things I hate about the boat is I have no time to myself."

He told Rebecca when she came for dinner, as had been her custom since the diagnosis, "Your mother and I are having the most intimate time of our lives. Nobody has any place to go. Nothing else to do." This time, I was protective and appreciative of that state. You, you, you. He often had said over the years, "You're always so busy." Meaning, why don't you spend more time with me? More than three meals a day. More than bed together at naptime and nighttime.

Years ago, that insatiability caused me to say one night over dinner, first reaching for his hand — our habit when we had something critical to say to the other, "Need doesn't feel like love. The result," I said, "is to make me feel like running away, not drawing close." "I'm so sorry," he said putting his other hand on top of mine. I asked him to list some things he loved about me. "I need to be reminded that you know the difference." In the ridiculous play of memory, all I could remember from the list was, "Your kissy lips."

Rebecca had the ability to laugh at him and get him to see the absurdity of his morose state in my absences. When the Times sent me on a solo drive the length of Patagonia from the sea to the Andes, he reported to her, "As usual, Gabriel has stopped eating. Every time she leaves, I have to get down on the floor and feed him. One peace of kibble at a time. I'm nearing that state myself."

"Oh, Dad. Eat your pasta. Have another vodka."

Yes, dying was intimate, and I drew close. We were single minded, welded together in the process of this long leave-taking.

Today in Central Park, party girl cherry trees took up their ridiculous dance to the rhythm of the wind. Show offs.

In spring we'd lived two lives and lived each with intensity. The life in the moment and the life of anticipation of summer when Bob could shake the chains, turn off the clock and hoist sail. Spring promised his deliverance.

The second summer after his death, when I'd moved into Bob's reconstructed office, from my window seat with its view down to the promenade and East River, I could see that everybody out there was having fun.

The party boats flowed with the river's mighty tide. Oh, happy, happy people. Shouts and laughs carried over the water and up eleven stories to my aerie, which more often than not had become a refuge of peace and light. From my bed I could see the moon at night, from my window seat, the Roosevelt Island lighthouse. I was very lucky. I acknowledged that every night before falling asleep and every morning upon waking. Grief hadn't killed gratitude.

It was summer and two cigarette boats raced each other. So

macho and young were their skippers. They didn't know their lives were running out like sand in an hourglass. They didn't know it was inevitable. Nor should they. It was right that on this summer night, they were free to rejoice in what was now. Speed. River scents. Muscular arms. The ability to get a hard on by the mere thought of a girl. Even as they raced across this cold water it could happen.

Why should they know on a careless summer eve that what lay ahead was loss followed by loss and then more loss? Nature's great gift — she doesn't show previews.

"I hate Sundays," a widow of three years told me. Our lives without our spouses brought us days and seasons we wished to flee. I hated summer. But it was in the nature of grief to be able to step aside on occasion, leaving room for delight. Whenever that happened, I thought of Gerald Stern's poem, "Lucky Life."

"Lucky life isn't one long string of horrors
and there are moments of peace, and pleasure, as I lie in between the blows."

There were times when I could grab hold of happiness between the blows, and times when I could delight in these evenings with their light gilded, brick buildings, and a breeze softened the harsh heat of day. There was no predicting the emotion served up at any particular moment.

Sometimes there were entire days of joy. A self-conscious joy but joy nonetheless. Before great sorrow we're happy without being in awe of the event. Happiness came and went like the tides, ho-hum.

When it came, I wanted to fall to my knees, "Thank you angel of happiness, God of the lark, the good laugh. Thank you for this visitation in the hour of our need."

Even with those unexpected interludes, summer required of me mental triathlon strength. I must swim! Oh, yes. I must! It's summer! A clambake! I tried to rally, to feign summer happiness. To join in the fun. But as darkness moved across the water, I didn't plunge ahead like the cigarette boat boys. Even as I knew living backwards was a crime against the day we're given, I ached for summers past.

Fireworks! July 4! Missing, missing, missing.

Labor Day brought relief. With fall, the days grew shorter and edged towards the cusp of melancholy. Monarch butterflies alighted on the buddleia bush, fueling up for their unlikely, diaphanous, winged flight three thousand miles to Mexico. Birdsong dimmed to mere murmurs.

Even the cheers of children in the surf were fainter as they propelled themselves into the dying of the days.

I relished autumn and its' shutting down of summer mania, snuffing out its expectations of energy and exaltation. I preferred fog and gales. Rain and snow. Weather that asked nothing of me.

February was the anniversary of the death month. The dirty, used up snow month. Citizens of this city became either defiant or depressed. The defiant chose to be triumphant in the face of this long, long, Thomas Hardy gray season. They forfeited their boots. They ignored their gloves. Others succumbed to gloom, convinced this would be the year spring did not come. The consumption of wine increased and started earlier. If admitted to Lenox Hill hospital due to alcohol poisoning, no one would hold it against them. It was February.

My spirits were light. They got better with each prediction of another storm heading our way. "More snow on Friday." "Sleet and rain on Tuesday." "Unusually cold." Bring on the bone-numbing blizzard. Blanket me beneath a gunmetal sky.

In this defeated atmosphere, I was free of summer's happy, happy volleyball on the beach, shrieks with the first dive into the sea.

And Spring with its insistence on celebration and a goat-footed balloon man was safely behind. In barren February, if any one said anything at all it was, "Will this winter never end?" Fine with me if it didn't.

A friend told me his psychiatrist once mused, "Depressed people like rainy days because they match their mood." How about those of us who aren't depressed but just plain sad? How about those of us who are matter of fact about our hearts failing to regain full range of motion?

Because pain obliterates perspective and forms a wall against optimistic thoughts about the future, I could not know that joy would reenter my life. I told a friend, "I've accepted that I'll never be happy again," and was surprised at my certainty that this was okay I no longer wished for happiness, only the absence of pain.

Those moments were sufficient. I was surprised when, on the first New Year's Eve alone, I announced to the dog lying next to my bed, the bed I hadn't burned, "This is enough. This is enough." Being warm and well fed, having a roof over my head was enough.

Don't count on it. After my proud pronouncement to the dog, at two in the morning, that hour which should forbid musing, I awakened to remembrance and longing for Bob's and my New Year's Eve ritual. The older three children would have returned home to their mother following Christmas in West Hartford with mine. Rebecca would be in bed when young and out when older. We celebrated being alone. We celebrated us. Caviar and blinis, icy vodka, and music. Bruckner, Buxtehude, Bach and Brahms, Vladimir Horowitz urging Scriabin to be born anew. We toasted our limitless blessings, the fact that we had found one another. "What were the chances…?"

We never stopped thanking whatever fates, forces, gods, stars, mysteries conspired to bring us together.

"Thank you."

"Thank you."

Stick Around This Year, Then You Can Do Whatever You Want

A WEEK BEFORE THE FIRST ANNIVERSARY of Bob's death, I was sitting at dinner when Gabriel walked in from the bedroom, put his head in my lap and cried.

I reached down to feel his stomach, a habit from the care of Bob. Pain? Is the stomach distended? Hard and enlarged? Yes. Gabriel's stomach felt to my hand as Bob's did in crisis. He looked at me. "Yes," I tell him. "I'll help you."

Into the car and to the Animal Medical Center. In the waiting room a couple was weeping next to an empty cat carrier. A cop smiled while talking to his German Shepherd K9 partner. This was the hour not of checkups but of emergencies, bad news, and off duty cops. I sat on the floor with Gabriel, my hand on his stomach, and as I had with Bob, willed it to transmit heat, to warm him, to ease his mounting torment.

"Ascher." I stood and urged Gabriel to do likewise. When that was impossible, the hefty vet tech approached and lifted him. As his biceps flexed I noticed a tattoo, "Irma." Really? Did anyone name girls Irma anymore? I was pondering this as he gestured to me to follow him to the examining room where a vet with a non-expression palpated his stomach. She sighed and said, "We'll have to keep him for the night." I put my head down on the dog's. "I'll see you in the morning. I'll be back. Promise."

The call came at 9 a.m. Cancer. Nothing to be done. I agreed to the recommended act of mercy scheduled for tomorrow morning. I called Tshering who loved him and had walked, fed and tended to him when I could not. Would she like to be with me? Yes.

We were shown to a room into which Gabriel was rolled on a gurney. "Hi, Sweetie,"

I smiled at him. The doctor said, "I'll give you as long as you need."

"I worry that he was so stoic. This must have been going on for quite a while."

"If he was stoic," said the doctor, "it's because he wanted to be."

Yes. I believed that of this dog. For all I knew, cancer had been eating within since the morning I'd asked him to stick around for the year. I met his dark eyes that stared into mine. Neither of us averted our gaze. His seemed to convey, "It's ok." Tshering held his paw and wept, "I'm quite certain he'll come back as a human."

I leaned down and breathed in his scent one last time, and whispered, "Thank you for holding up your end of the bargain."

The Value of Routine

WHAT I HELD ONTO, clung to were the remains of a former routine as I struggled to create a new post-Bob, post Gabriel version. There's so much to be said for routine's orderly weavings and repetitions.

It may be an essential element of sanity. Like ritual, routine controls the chaos of the mind. The sister-in-law of a recovering alcoholic told me that he advised others in recovery, "First thing you do in the morning is make your bed." When someone he sponsors calls in crisis, his first question is, "Did you make your bed?" Grab the day before it grabs you. Prius carpe diem quam dies carpat te.

Once Rebecca was grown and gone, tending to Bob, the dog and writing chapters, articles and columns were the perimeters of my routine. Every weekday make breakfast, brush teeth, choose a tie. Kiss kiss. Out he went at eight.

The days flowed with a certain grace. Call to check in during ten-minute breaks between patients. 10 a.m.-10:10 a.m., 11a.m.-11:10 a.m.

1 p.m. Key in door. "Ain't ya hungry?" You bet. Lunch on the table by 1:10. In bed together for a twenty minute nap before the first afternoon patient. "All it takes is one dream to make me fresh for the afternoon." Or on occasion, all it took was a sweet interlude of love until the alarm sounded.

Break 4:00 p.m.-4:10 p.m. Break 5:00 p.m.-5:10. Call. Talk. Laugh. Share.

Finish at 7 p.m. One more dog walk. Day was done.

"Without work, I would have lost my mind," asserted two friends whose wives had predeceased them. Each continued the routine of some forty years — rising with the alarm, shaving, breakfasting, suiting up. Out into the day, into the flow of humanity, to the bus, the subway, through the park.

Off to the office. Lunch dates. "Please check my calendar…" Routine takes charge when mind and heart fail. It carries within it a sense of obligation. Others are setting their watches by it.

The disciplined can count on self-perpetuated routines. "I just do it, it's a habit."

"I run on the treadmill for 30 minutes when I get home from work. Don't even think about it. It's a habit."

"Floss? First thing in the morning, then I don't have to do it before bed when I'm tired. An old habit from childhood."

"Lose keys? No need if you develop the habit of putting them in your right coat pocket. Then that's where they'll always be."

I didn't ask about summer. What did one do in summer when there was no coat pocket? I didn't belabor the pocket-less curse of women's clothing.

Bob's and my routines served us well except for the routine of anger when I accepted the writing assignments to the far, isolated reaches of the world. My favorites.

Then we fought with such intensity you would have thought he was Israel and I, Palestine. What else are battles about if not boundaries? Mine! Mine! Mine!

My right to be independent. His right to want me by his side. We held those rights to be self-evident when in fact they were no more than whims with long histories.

He tried to draw parallels that would help me understand how it felt to be "abandoned." "How would you feel if I told you I was going to sail in the Bermuda race?"

"Thrilled for you."

And I would have been. As I delighted in my assignments. I had a passion for the craft that demanded observing close and deep. I thrilled to the challenge of bringing a place to life for the reader, describing scenes in a new way even if they had been written about many times. Venice. Paris. The Amalfi Coast. The sea. Are you kidding? Best of all was the sense of handing a gift to someone who could not be where I was but could feel that they were. Being on assignment made me feel alive. Something worth fighting for.

Did I miss him when I was away? Of course. Once when in Rome for The Times, as I gazed up at the Sistine Chapel ceiling, at God's and Adam's urgent and vain reach for each other's hands, I extended mine and closed on emptiness. I'd forgotten he wasn't there. The hand I reached for in poignancy was an ocean away. I was practicing. Missing him was part of the practice.

I didn't realize then that loss doesn't respond to rehearsal. How could I have known? I'd never had a husband die.

That our love survived his separation anxiety and my insistence on independence spoke to its enduring strength. While there might be hysteria, outrage, hurt feelings, spilled tears, love held firm. Even when I didn't like him.

Now there was no routine to shatter. Scattered were the ashes of structure. Silenced were the skirmishes.

There were times I regretted leaving my former office job structured around the demands of others. What had been so awful about being a lawyer? Hadn't it been better than being here alone, left to my own devices to sleep until cured? Hadn't it been better to have a place where I was expected to show up, follow instructions, work too hard and too long writing briefs and memos in preparation for litigation?

I'd decided to go to law school when I was 30 and caught up in the spirit of the Women's Movement, President Johnson's Great Society and Civil Rights. "Making a difference," was the cry of the day and I was just young enough and the times eruptive enough for me to believe that was a possibility. It was a short-lived career because I disliked being a Wall Street lawyer, a path that I'd been told was the first step in becoming a Constitutional lawyer. "Go and get your training, then you can do good," was the received wisdom. That training involved the defense of large corporations and those charged with white color crimes. It was so antithetical to my nature, I couldn't stay the course, went back home and resumed writing and this time there were publishers.

I tried to honor aspects of Bob's and my old routine. Every night, I set the table, made dinner, sat down, poured wine and raised my glass. "To love," I'd say aloud. I continued to squeeze the morning orange juice, make coffee, eat a full breakfast of eggs and toast. I attempted to read the Times addressed to Bob that kept showing up on the floor outside the front door as though two of us were still within, ready to discuss the editorial. "You be in charge of foreign, I'll do domestic."

I no longer got up every morning at 6:30 because if sleep came, I loathed disrupting it. I didn't listen from the bed as he turned on the radio to hear if the world was still here. I knew the answer to that. The air was still with absence.

In the first month following the death, I was anxious for more work to fill the gaps. I needed an organizing principle. A deadline that was not a death line. I was so caught in desperation that between assignments I called an editor who was a friend of a friend, someone for whom I'd never worked. We're sorry. She's not in the office. She's on a shoot.

"Would you like her cell number?"

"Yes, please."

Too bad for her. She answered.

"My husband just died. I need work. Will you give me an assignment?"

Her voice was kind. She gave no sign that she heard a mad woman on the other end of the phone. Of course. She would keep me in mind. I never heard from her. Of course.

A routine dictated by madness could not hold. A routine created out of despair would burn itself to embers and grow cold.

When the kind widowers told me that without their regular jobs and the attendant collegiality, they would have lost their minds, I didn't tell them I had lost mine.

Sometimes it Slaps You

FOR YEARS, grief remained one step ahead of me. I regarded it as the enemy, a rival in a death match. A prankster, it had taken up residence and hovered, ready to strike, reminding me of Shelley's, "Death... laughs at our despair." There's a whole lot of laughing going on.

When dogs pick up the scent of a sick and dying dog, it is not unusual for them to try to take it down. Or so, I'm told and so I have witnessed. Survival of the fittest. I must remain alert and fit. Have no doubt. It has taken out those stronger than I.

I dropped my guard one night three years into widowhood. I was minding my own business at home with Seamus Heaney's translation of Antigone, fresh pasta, a vodka and tonic. Perfect. Weather cool. Bee Balm and Butterfly Bush on the terrace in bloom. At ease, I opened the book and bam! Two lines — "Love like a green fern shading/The cheek of a sleeping girl" delivered a punch to the gut. I sat back to catch my breath but, there it came again and finished the job.

In the fall after his and Rebecca's college graduation and before Chuck entered medical school, he taught third grade in an inner city school. "I want to give back to education before I spend more money on my own." Yes, Chuck talked like that and acted like that. His low key, direct kindness and firmness worked with the kids. So much so that when he told the class that he was going to marry Rebecca, he received a note from one of the children, "Mr. Walsh. I want to marry you but I be a boy."

And there were those who didn't want to marry him. One was

the class troublemaker. Chuck upon reporting his latest shenanigans to the boy's mother was told, "I'm going to slap him upside the head."

Grief slaps us upside the heart. Last week, I was driving upstate happy in an apple blossom flecked day, singing along with Dionne Warwick on the radio, "Walk on by…" And then the wrong song came on — Herb Alpert singing, "This Guy's in Love with You."

Entirely the wrong song playing just when I'd told my psychic sentinels they could take a break. All's quiet, go get yourselves some lunch.

"You see this guy, this guy's in love with you…"

This song had always moved us to hold each other close as we danced in the kitchen.

Off with the radio.

I'd thought I was safe driving through bucolic countryside. There was no safety. It was all a fiction.

I told myself, I can do this. It's just a song. No, I can't.

"Say you're in love… if not

I'll just die."

And he did, didn't he? The guy who was in love died.

Cursed Beauty

AND IT SLAPPED ME upside the heart the first year as I stood before the pyrotechnics of a Maui sunset.

What was I thinking when I accepted the offer to teach at a weeklong writers' conference? I wasn't. It was that fire beneath my feet that brought me here. Don't think, just go. Say yes to everything.

I liked to teach, delighted when promise was revealed. But Maui? No, that became clear. Too far from home and too far from more subdued land and seascapes.

How was I to know there would be so much reckless beauty? I hated the island's blood soaked, evening skies, the Pacific's responding violent violet. I hated its expanse of stone free, white beaches, its trails through fawning, florid fauna.

This place could cut out your heart and toss it into the sea.

Why hadn't I headed for the cold regions and their bland palettes? Lapland, for instance. Because no one in Lapland offered a round trip ticket plus room and board. That's why. So, here I was — precisely where I should not be.

Did the scent of death still cling to me? Why else did the other writers teaching here avoid me?

At this conference, I was relegated to the edge of the playground. The "regulars," those who taught here every year banded together. This famous novelist ate her meals at a table with that famous novelist. Two guys whose names meant nothing to me but appeared to be the organizer's pets sat with a renowned mystery writer. Everybody wanted to sit with another novelist who was relishing a recent, surprise success and rave reviews. She and I shared an agent. As we stood in the cafeteria line, I told her this. "Oh, yes?" She helped herself to the bean salad and moved along.

There were empty seats at their tables but nobody invited me to join and I lacked the self-confidence to do so even without an invitation. Day after day. Meal after meal. Even as I sat alone at a table for six. All the other tables would fill with writers who'd been on the New York Times bestseller list.

I called Rebecca from my small, dark, hotel room. Who knew there was a dark hotel room in Maui? Well, this was Marriot against nature and Marriot won. Brown rug, walls and draperies. I described the scene to her and confessed, "I'm dreading breakfast."

"You're kidding, right Mom?"

She was familiar with the independent, adventuresome version of her mother. The mother who when writing a travel article would drive alone the length of Patagonia, the mother who when writing for the Times about Death Valley would take an extra day when a ranger invited her to ride a horse leading two mules into that valley's uncharted territory to pick up two cartographers and bring them out.

They'd been there for two-weeks and were a bit wild-eyed. "Phew! We thought you'd never come."

The mother who would eat alone in restaurants.

"No, I'm not kidding. I feel like the new girl in a class of sixth grade mean girls."

"Here's what you do," she advised. "Pretend that I'm with you and sleeping late. Go to breakfast alone. You do that all the time when we travel together. Pretend that after breakfast, you're coming back to the room to get me so we can go for coffee."

When I became a mother, I wanted to be what I thought mothers should be. Those to whom offspring turned for guidance, wisdom and comfort. First the lap, then the wisdom.

I had been secure in the lap stage but often flummoxed in the latter. As the mother of an adult, I strived but feared that too often I stumbled and fell, failing to be centered, steady and wise. But, I was grateful for this call even as I knew she needed a strong surviving parent, not a wounded bird.

When my father died, my mother's grief made her blind to her daughter's. I vowed not to be like that. My hubris was in direct proportion to my inexperience. Hubris is always in direct proportion to inexperience.

Rebecca's sisters and brother loved their father and suffered the loss, but grief is intensely private. They knew I loved them and was standing by, but I couldn't presume to know how they felt. Feelings were complicated by the contradictions in his personality formerly unchecked by a secure marriage. He lost his way and temper to a degree not suffered by Rebecca. Which is not to say he did not lose his temper. He could be a mad man. But in him she had an ally. She could turn to one of us when the other made her miserable. The other three children lacked that buffer. They bore the wounds of divorce and separation. Their love for their father was strong, ambivalent and angry. Their loss was terrible and fraught with pain. This was the second time he'd left them.

I was not to forget that. I was not, I told myself, to become so mired in my misery that I failed to acknowledge theirs.

But I struggled to corral grief within the confines of my home. As if such a thing were possible. I reeked of it. It seeped from my pores leaving a slug-like trail. And here I was in Maui and the other "kids" weren't being nice to me and I was lonely and my daughter advised, "Here's what you do."

Was this right? Was this correct? I floundered. I adored her. She had her father's saber-like clarity and short fuse. We were different and I admired her more direct responses rather than my musings, which were never Bob and Rebecca's way. But, our way as a family was to stick close to one another. We were a tight unit at the ready when one of us "lost our shit," as Rebecca described it.

We defended and explained each other. It was lonely for both of us not having Bob as our ally.

When she was in the throes of adolescence and could, according to her, "feel the surge of hormones coming on," know trouble was coming. One such time, I was the target and lashed out in kind. She went into her father's dressing room in tears and I heard her say, "She's such a bitch." Bob's response was, "I know, sweetie but she's our bitch and we love her."

Perfect. Her feelings were acknowledged and in one short exchange he let her know it was o.k. to be furious with me at that moment, knowing the love was steadfast. One did not exclude the other. We did that for each other.

When we failed as a unit it was when both Bob and Rebecca needed me simultaneously. The one whose needs were not met felt cast out. Too often, I responded to Bob's for the sake of the marriage, determining that was best for the family, for a harmonious unit that could support a child. But I believe I'm in the company of many parents when I suffer nocturnal l'esprit de l'escaliers. Those, if-I-had-it-to-do-again thoughts. We don't have it to do again.

After Awhile

I CALLED UPON the old, familiar sense of adventure and called Gourmet Magazine to tell an editor that I was planning to drive to Appalacia in search of a quilter. I told her why. Would they like a story? Yes, sure. And so, I hit the road and headed south in an old car with a new dog and a trunk full of Bob's bow ties, shirts, and boxer shorts. I was on a mission to find someone who would stitch these remnants of a life into quilts for our children so when pulling up the covers on cold winter nights, they might be in a semblance of their father's once embrace.

My cotton cargo consisted of floral prints, pastel stripes, solid blues, a frivolous pink and white dress shirt I'd bought Bob when on assignment in Venice. I'd reasoned that maybe if upon return, I threw gifts in the door ahead of myself they would deflate the she-left-me sulk.

Each item of clothing was saturated with memory. The morning ritual. "Will you help me pick out a bow tie?" We'd peruse the rack of some hundred my mother had made for him over the years. Every Christmas they shared the delight as he opened a box that held three or four or six, each brighter and more playful than the next. Blush red peonies, yellow daisies, lavender generics.

Out he would go into the morning and the day's work looking, I always thought like the most attractive man on earth.

"You look so handsome."

"You just say that because you love me."

We were both right.

I travelled along the Shenandoah River on serpentine Route 50, dubbed the "Loneliest Highway." That seemed about right.

My ultimate destination Floyd, Virginia a speck on the map of Appalachia where during the last year of WW II my mother and I'd lived with my paternal grandparents while awaiting my father's discharge from the army. His father owned the sawmill where upon his return, he worked for as long as he could stand working for that hot-tempered, hard drinking man. Until he'd saved enough money to support us when we moved to Delaware, Ohio so he could return to college on the G.I. Bill.

I recalled remnants of my first three years in Floyd, or thought I did. Childhood viewed in retrospect, through the scrim of sentimentality serves up lovely if inaccurate pictures. Mine were of quilts hanging from clotheslines, crocks of sweet butter and bottles of thick, yellow cream carried from a springhouse. Rows of Mason jars filled with green beans, beets, and apple butter. Baskets of steaming biscuits.

After six hours of driving, I was delighted when I saw a Pepto Bismal pink diner with turquoise trim and a sign outside that said, "Elvis Fans Parking. Violators will be all shook up." How could I resist? I parked as a fan. Naturally.

I opened the door for Hugo, the standard poodle I'd gotten a few months after Gabriel's death. I had needed something to move the air in my too still apartment where there was no more eager approach, no wagging tale, no dutiful circling of the dog bed once, twice, three times before settling down. Stillness is something we seek when life is too full of itself. In death it hangs as heavy as a rebuke.

He bounded out with puppy exuberance. Air! Animal scents! After sufficient sniffing and peeing, he was returned to the car and I went inside. I ordered The Pink Cadillac Diner's specialty chili then leaned back in the booth and admired the 1950s movie posters, the 1938 flathead Harley propped in a corner, the plush pink "needlepoint" rug bearing Elvis' likeness.

A Platters record slipped into place in the old jukebox. "Deep in the dark your kiss will thrill me, like days of old…" Time to leave. How to explain the tears?

"I'm so sorry. I've got to go." Echoes of fleeing C.V.S. and Andy Williams.

In a few hours, I arrived in Floyd. I'd learned from many assignments that the first stops in making acquaintance with a place are the barbershop and the place the regulars eat.

I parked and entered the former with its one barber chair and four men waiting or just gathering to gossip and laugh together. The one whose head the barber's sheers were clipping turned to look at Hugo and said, "That dog won't hunt." I liked this place. "True but he'll eat and so will I. Where do you guys go for lunch?" It was unanimous. "The Blue Ridge Diner right across from the red, brick courthouse with the Confederate soldier out front. You won't have no trouble finding it." To make sure that was the case, one of the men walked me to the door and pointed to the landmarks. "Got it. Thank you. I'll come back when the dog needs a haircut."

I tied Hugo outside, apologizing that he might be the brunt of more jokes and walked in to take a seat at one of ten Formica topped tables set on a beige linoleum floor. I eavesdropped — a great resource for a writer — on bits of conversation between the waitress and an old man in bib overalls. As she handed him the bill she said, "You give my love to Elma, you hear?" When she approached, retrieving her pad from her apron pocket and the stub of a pencil from behind her ear, I ordered the special of the day — grilled cheese sandwich and tomato soup. $3.00. No need to write that down. The sandwich arrived on white bread fried in butter. Ask for multi-grain and you might be laughed out of town. The soup was as good as, maybe even better than the Campbell's Mom served us when we were kids. "Well, now, honey, 'at's exactly what h'it is." The waitress introduced herself, "Iris Yates, and you are?"

Now that we knew each other's names, she continued with details of the soup. Butter and cream. Lots of both." High in fat, low on pretension. Mourners' preferred cuisine.

The large biscuits on my plate ("catheads") were golden outside and white as paper within, a sure sign that they were made from Virginia's Best, the local ("down yonder ta Elliston") self-rising flour bleached to a white unseen in nature. Even fresh snow isn't this white.

"Don't never use nothin' else."

To write in the dialect of another is frowned upon by those who consider it condescending rather than celebrating. 'S'all they know. Other than recording, how else to keep a language and its utterances alive before we cease sounding not of our place but of no place? Until we speak in the language of sit-coms? This was the lyrical speech that still resonated with the Scotch Irish lilt of the area's early settlers. History kept alive. Music to my ears.

As were Mrs. Yates instructions for making biscuits. "I jes' grabs some Crisco an' sweet milk an' work it into the flour. Course you gotta warsh yer hands first. Then, jes' work hit real good, pat hit likey so, then roll 'em out, cut em and bake at 500 degrees fer thirteen minutes." These days I'd developed a heightened sense of gratitude for moments of happiness. This was one.

Thus, equipped with the requisite knowledge for a life in biscuit baking and directions to a quilting source, I paid, thanked Ida, and got back in the car to head for School House Fabrics. Housed within a turn of the century, former grammar school it was a pilgrimage site for quilters of the South.

The quilts I saw there had been pieced on sewing machines. No. I wanted what my grandmother would have made for me if she were alive.

Did anyone around here still do that? A conference among the salesclerks resulted in a name. "Mrs. Duncan on Alum Ridge Road 's the only one quiltin' by hand." They offered a number and a heavy, black, rotary phone. When a soft voice answered I explained my mission and told her the School House ladies had given me her number. She gave directions and suggested I come over so she could see what I had.

The narrow, two-lane, switchback road to my destination wound around a mountain, then back on itself. At the site of a 180-degree curve, there was a sign, "Are you prepared to meet God?" I made a note to think about that as I entered the next hairpin.

Uldine Duncan lived in a four-room house as tiny and neat as its occupant. Each gray curl on her head appeared crafted. Artisanal hair. She rocked in her chair to the rhythm of our slow, quiet conversation. "Thems that makes quilts on machines...I hain't got nothin' agin 'em but you might as well jes' go to the store an' buy yerself one."

Although she feared her stitching days were numbered, she held up gnarled, arthritic fingers to make the point and sighed, "Well, lemme see what you've got." When I opened the trunk, she reached for a bow tie and eyed it professionally. I was relieved by her cold appraisal. She'd seen husbands come and go. These mountains were hard on the very young and very old. What was one more dead husband? Yet again I'd been given the gift of context. It put things in perspective. I began to see the clothing for what it was and would become rather than a reminder of what was gone.

Yes, she'd give it a try. She'd let me know when they were done.

No receipt, no money changed hands. What was one more dead husband?

Transitions

THERE WAS AN ADDITIONAL MOTIVE for leaving home. After a year of saying, yes to everything, I began to feel an unease with transitions. I wanted to defy it and reasoned that the cure might lie in being the instigator of change rather than its victim.

I lacked the grace I hoped might come with years of studying Buddhism. I had failed to learn to "let go." I held tight. All those teachings, all that meditation and I'd gone into reverse. Thank you so much, you can have your impermanence. Even though a Tibetan lama told me shortly after Bob's death, "The good thing about impermanence is that suffering is impermanent, also." I thought, "There is good impermanence and bad impermanence." I was a living example of how we create our own suffering. Good impermanence, bad impermanence. Nonsense. I clasped these concepts even as I knew they meant nothing.

Even the smallest change could set anxiety in motion, causing emotional whiplash as the present zoomed past and deserted me.

I grew anxious when I packed and homesick before I'd crossed the bridge out of the city. I cleaned the apartment before departures. Should an ill fate befall me, I didn't want Rebecca to have to cope with a mess. In addition to the mess of death.

When leaving for my writers' room at the library after crossing my apartment's threshold and pulling the door shut, I'd reopen it, reenter to make certain I'd turned off the gas, the water. One-step forward, one step back. And so it would be until there were two steps forward and one back.

Leave takings teetered on the edge of sorrow. If I'd spent a weekend with Rebecca's family and stayed behind for an extra day in the country, the moment I heard their car pull out of the drive heading back to the city, I knew I'd made a mistake. Their absence began to pulsate in the air. Spaces left behind exert energy.

My first widowhood beau (ridiculous but what else to call a sixty-year-old gentleman caller?) grew impatient with my unwillingness to make future dates. Dread approached when he'd say, "Look at your calendar." No! No! I don't want to look at my calendar. Dates, plans, time are fictions we create to make us feel we're in charge here. Nobody's in charge. We're just floating in space until snatched away.

Each parting could be weighty with intimations of death. Each transition a miniature death. Goodbye to that moment.

I know. I know. We are all transients just passing through. But sometimes, it's rough terrain.

Gentlemen Callers

THAT FIRST SUITOR (another quaint sobriquet) promised to smooth the ride. Thus, how could I say no to a dinner invitation? An invitation that held the possibility of diversion and a momentary easing of grief's grip. "Say yes to everything."

I was not constricted by the protocol required of the "ideal" Civil War widow who was to wear black, to mourn (quietly and privately) for a minimum of two and a half years, to resign herself to God's will, focus on her children, devote herself to her husband's memory, and if she were Confederate, to his cause. Flirting was absolutely outside the pale.

I didn't hesitate, considering it "too soon," because I didn't understand that this was a date. The idea of dating scared me. "What's it like, now?" I'd asked a friend twenty years younger than I, "They don't expect you to go to bed on the first date, do they?"

"Well, not on the first..."

"If it's going well, would it be like... after a month or two of dating?"

"Maybe you're not ready for this."

"I'm not ready for this."

I didn't worry because this man had been one of Bob's favorite doctors. We'd been moved by his kindness, humor and generosity. He made house calls, which had contributed to our not needing hospice. When Bob became too ill to leave home for chemotherapy treatments, this man arranged for them to be administered at home. He respected my determination to have this time with Bob divorced from clinical surroundings.

One evening when he made a house call, Bob told him the story of our love affair. It was his favorite story and like all those retold over a long time it had taken on a mythic quality.

"I fell in love with her the minute I saw her."

"Why?"

"Because she was kind to children."

I'd never heard him state such a succinct reason. It can take a lifetime with a person to make any sense of how and why love was born. Thus, the myth, a way of explaining the inexplicable. The mystery held in reverence.

After a dinner of easy conversation, when Dr. P dropped me off at my apartment building he asked, "When can I see you again?"

"Oh, there's not need to do that."

"Do what?"

"Take your patient's widow out more than once." I'd assumed this was what he did as a matter of course. A long food line of the bereft.

"You think that's what this was?"

"It's lovely that you do that."

He laughed, "Thank you but that's not what this was."

"What was it?"

"A date."

Well, that was easy.

And I did see him again and again and again because all the qualities Bob and I had admired held true as I got to know him better. And we had fun. But, how could it not have been too soon? How could anyone withstand the ferocity of my ongoing passion for the man I'd married?

And yet while it lasted, going out with him was preferable to staying put with the single objective of proving to myself that I could still breathe, then taking a sleeping pill to pull a curtain down over the empty side of my bed. On the other side of the open door was a kind man holding out a hand and the possibility of touch thawing my body frozen in the ice of abstinence.

On the sixth date, I didn't say no.

I didn't say, don't desire me, don't let me experience desire; don't awaken my body to what it once was.

I said, yes.

I was drawn to this man's tenderness and sincerity. He gave me a gift short of resurrection, he made me laugh. He returned me to the ordinary world where people were falling in love, having their hearts broken, arguing about politics, going to the theater, deciding what to have for dinner. People who lived as though they didn't know life was a minefield.

We traveled to France and Spain and Ireland. We looked at art and made love and drank wine and laughed and laughed and laughed.

And he said, "I do not think you are a happy person."

And I said, "I mourn my husband's death."

Widowed himself, he tried to make room for that. He tried to understand that ours was a ménage a trois. In the end, he could not. And why should he have?

He wanted a love of his own. He wanted me to love him for who he was, not as means of escape from the pain of grief, the fear of living a long time alone.

Oh, there were many reasons why it couldn't work. Although it worked it's purpose out over the course of a year. I did not love his criticism of my method of thinking, more meandering than the linear reasoning honed by his profession. He didn't love my not infrequent change of plans, my lack of attention to appearance. "Do you think it's alright to wear a bikini at your age?" Clearly, I did since I'd just come out of the ocean in one. "Bad hair day." Unlike his late wife, I didn't have a standing, weekly appointment with the hairdresser. But then his wife wore proper dresses and heels even at home.

We were both missing what we had lost and hoping that

someone could fill that gap, like a piece that fit into a jigsaw puzzle.

Rebecca was not enthusiastic. He had failed to save her father. He was nothing like her father. He wasn't her father. I couldn't disagree that he lacked Bob's elegance and far-ranging intelligence, his knowledge of history, music, literature, his insights into the human psyche. He had none of Bob's ferocious commitment to justice and equality in a world losing its way.

And although I could understand her response, I wanted to say, "I am just trying to hold myself together. I need this." But I didn't say that and it would have made no difference. "Mom, you can always have another husband, I can't have another father."

In spite of my complaints, I appreciated his attention and affection. I had assumed nobody would love me again, that for the rest of my life I'd be alone on Saturday nights. And here was a man who filled my Saturday nights, who observed closely to discover what pleased me and would deliver it. A surprise night at the opera, something that would not have been his choice. A plot of land on his property where I could plant a garden. In spite of what he considered to be my shortcomings, he loved me and delivered me to the widow's promised land — sexuality.

And so, I was loath to say goodbye. Another goodbye? Oh no. Not another goodbye.

Yes. Another goodbye once the passage of time had delivered me to firmer ground. I said, "Goodbye." He said, "No."

I said, goodbye.

He said, no.

I said goodbye.

Three months later, I accepted a friend's introduction to a smart, attractive widower. "You'll like him. He's a brilliant physicist."

At our first dinner together, when he rested his elbow on the table and his shirtsleeve slid back to reveal his wrist, I fell in love with it. The wrist. He, like Bob, was a left-handed tennis player. I fell in love with his serving wrist because it resembled Bob's.

I was not unaware of the lunacy of this, I thought of Eric Rohmer's 1970 movie "Claire's Knee" in which a man about to be married to someone else, falls in love with a teenager. Or more precisely, with her knee.

You'll-think-you're-sane-but-you're-not had morphed into, you'll–think-you're-sane-so-why-not? I proceeded in spite of anxiety's low hum. I was still riding grief's emotional rollercoaster and this carnival had offered me ten rides for the price of one. A close out sale for good reason. Sex! He lacked lust. Companionship! He was uncomfortable with intimacy.

I tried to convince myself I could live an exclusively cerebral life. We would sustain ourselves on lofty conversation. When alone, I could read Balli Kaur Jawswal's *Erotic Stories for Punjabi Widows.*

I considered myself drawing closer to old age. Wasn't a compromised life with the Man-With-the-Wrist preferable to signing up for Internet dating? Aging widow keeps a tidy room. Doesn't take up too much space. Will cook and clean.

Try as I might to sublimate my sexuality, he sensed it and it frightened him. "No, no, it's fine really." It would have been disaster and he knew it. The inevitable, "Let's meet for drinks," call. The inevitable, "You're a wonderful person but..." call. And then the words so chilling, they should be banned from break ups. "This isn't working out." He was quick to add, "But my analyst is away for the month." It was August after all. "And I can't make a decision without him." Really?

I wished him well. I left my dry martini, straight up, three olives behind. I unlocked my bike and as I got on, he asked, "Will you be okay riding home?"

"Mom, you aren't crying over this man," Rebecca said when I called to tell her. She'd been a fan until growing wary with the passage of time and my, "Nope, none" to her forthright questions about the sex. Following his return from a two-week business trip in India, she was shocked when the answer was the same. "Mom!

He should have had you up against the wall the minute you walked in!" "I didn't walk in. He wanted to meet on the street." No, he wasn't an up-against-the-wall kind of guy.

When I first started dating, I called my stepchildren to let them know, Lizzie's response was to cry with relief. "I've been so worried about your being lonely." When I told her about this breakup, she said, "Barbie, don't expect him to fill the holes in your heart. And don't blame him for not loving you the way Dad did, as though his life depended on it."

She was right. Of course, she was right. So many holes.

I asked my twenty-four-year-old Goddaughter whose experience was far greater than mine, "After a break-up, how long do you feel like shit?"

My dating had been limited to Bob and the first post-Bob gentlemen caller. A virgin twice removed

"A long time," said she.

A long time to fill the holes. One small, plastic beach shovel at a time.

Community

IN THE THIRD YEAR, Dorian who owned the fish store on York Avenue and had been selling me fish for thirty years, said while bringing a cleaver down on a salmon's glassy-eyed head, "Mrs. Ascher, a nice man, about sixty years old just came to buy fish. He told me he'd recently moved to the neighborhood and wanted to open an account. When I was taking down the information, I saw that his address was the same as yours!" My fish monger matchmaker. "I said to him, 'You should meet Barbara Ascher. You can't miss her. She's got a big, black standard poodle.'"

She wrapped a slick filet in white paper, tied it with string and handed it to me.

"How do you know he's single?"

She ignored the question. "He's good looking. And he was buying fish, not prepared food. That's good."

Buying fish. All right then.

"He's probably gay," was Rebecca's response when I told her.

I was a fraud. This always happened when I got to the part of the story where I determined the single life was the only life for me, high ho! In the lobby and elevator, I began to watch for a man matching Dorian's description, a man carrying fish who was new to the building.

Just when I'd convinced myself that my libido had been tucked in and gone to sleep, I found myself following an attractive, tall, straight-spined man to the back of the 79th Street Crosstown Bus where I stood reading Foreign Policy over his shoulder, ready should he want to strike up a conversation. He didn't.

In the morning I'd been singing, "Don't Fence Me In." In the evening while walking Hugo, I saw a man walking a similar poodle. He said, "Aren't they great dogs?" I agreed and noticed how good-looking he was. I dawdled just in case he had more to say. "Have a good day," said he and was off.

When Dr. P's demands for time had begun to make me feel as though the walls were closing in, I'd told him that "Don't Fence Me In" was my theme song. I sang a few bars for good measure. "Who knows? I might become a Buddhist nun." I meant it. I might. He didn't understand my need for space, time, solitude. I tried to avoid using the word "space" as in, "I need space." I tried not to be a cliché. Good luck with that.

"There's been a shift," I told my friend Lily, widowed six months after I. I described it to her, trying to shine a glimmer of light into the fog of her sadness. "It happens and it feels as though the plates of the earth have shifted." I described how the sorrow was loosening as was some of grief's heavy insistence.

She didn't know what the hell I was talking about.

I told her about my dating adventures. "But this shift has resulted in many nights when I prefer being at home with a book rather than out to dinner with a man."

Men and women alike, friends who had met Dr. P commented, "Do you know how hard it is to find a good man? Let alone one who is kind and caring and who loves you?"

What if I didn't want to find a good man? What if I didn't want to find any man at all? Now that being alone was becoming not a condition to be cured, but robust independence, I was discovering there were many ways to love. To love without grabbing hold. Friends, work, one's existence. Which is not to say that there weren't those occasional nights when I'd see myself as an old woman alone at 5 p.m. sitting in the local coffee shop, crumbling Saltines into my split pea soup and putting the remaining, unopened pack in my purse. Night after night. And so it went, that third year.

Depression

IT WAS JULY 4TH and I'd chosen to stay at home alone. In the pre-dawn, the early hours of vivid dreams when consciousness hovers between the two worlds of wakefulness and somnolence, Bob was back.

Not in the way he had appeared on other nights when his arrival confused and disturbed. In those dreams, the children and I reviewed each step from diagnosis to death certificate losing our way trying to follow the evidence. How could we have been so wrong? How could the doctors have been so wrong? In those dreams, he would stand smiling among us as my bewilderment gave way to panic, as though I were struggling with an insoluble exam equation.

In those dreams my consternation was caused by confusion. How was I to explain without hurting his feelings that I thought he was dead? What a terrible thing to say to your husband. And what was I to say about the other man? How to confess infidelity? How were he and I to live in my small apartment? There wasn't room for both of us here.

When I awakened from such dreams, I welcomed the light of day and clarity.

But this July 4th visitation was different. It didn't exist in the dream world. This was real. We were laughing together sharing the intimacy of a private joke. I inhaled his scent. We stood at the bar at Sant Ambroeus and as my right arm pressed against his left, I felt the soft, well-worn fabric of his familiar navy blue and red-checked, cotton shirt. I heard the clink of our cups against the saucers, the sound of his voice as he spoke to the young, Italian man behind the bar who had been making our cappuccinos for such a long time, he'd invited us to attend his wedding.

I tasted the coffee, the best in New York. I noted how it never failed. I felt the foam against my upper lip and lifted my napkin to dab it. Bob took out his brown wallet stuffed with credit and ID cards, cash and favorite family photos, the children posed on the Paint Box steps, me grinning at him from a Caribbean beach. He pulled out two dollars, 30%. "They work so hard." He placed them on the bar. "Thank you so much." "Ciao." "Ciao." Out the door holding hands. There was always that magnetic, unthinking pull towards one another.

As we often did, we agreed to run our separate errands on this stretch of Madison Avenue between 77th and 81st Streets. I, uptown to buy a book, he three blocks down to buy batteries. "I'll meet you back at the car," I said. "I'll be right back," said he.

Returning ahead of him, I leaned against the car, to feel the sun's warmth on my face as I read. After six pages, I looked down the avenue in the direction he'd gone. It was taking him too long. There were lots of pedestrians enjoying the cloudless day but no Bob. He was always easy to spot because of his height and catching sight of him had never ceased to delight me. To cause a slight skip of the heart.

Anxiety grew. Where was he? Why was it taking so long?

I awakened to the awful truth. He wasn't meeting me back at the car. He wasn't meeting me anywhere. Ever. I wanted to rip the word "never" from the pages of dictionaries, from human tongues.

I opened my eyes to the sunlight coming through the window and then darkness closed in, pressing from above and pulling from below. And then I saw a black freight train, darker than Sargent's Venetian black broke through the living room wall and bore down on me.

I'd never had this experience, but I knew what it was. This was not grief. This was a different beast. I was caught on the tracks and my soul was about to be flattened like a penny. This was depression. Unlike grief, this had no purpose other than annihilation.

I pushed my arms and hands into the mattress to force myself from the bed. I thought that if I stood and faced the train head on, I might be saved. But I couldn't move. It was as though I'd been bound in chains. I continued to struggle against them and managed to lift myself upright into the darkness closing around me. I spoke to Hugo, "This is scary." And, as though he were capable of hospital corners, I said, "Let's make the bed. Let's try to act normal."

So, I did try to act normal as I called Rebecca, my only friend in town this Fourth of July weekend.

"May I take you out for breakfast?" I asked. "Great, of course." I suggested we meet at the Barking Dog café where we could eat outside in the company of our dogs. "Twenty minutes?" "Perfect."

When I arrived, she was waiting. She was always on time. I rarely was. It had long been a bone of contention. But not today. She knew from my voice that I was in trouble.

We ordered, and I began to describe the episode. She asked, "Why did you get out of bed?"

"Because I was too scared to stay there."

"Don't be such a Puritan. Depressed people take to their beds all the time."

Alice James came to mind.

"When you leave here, how do you plan to spend the day?"

"Reading Andrew Solomon's, *Noonday Demon*."

"Mom!" She said in a tone familiar to any mother of grown children. A combination of exacerbation and certainty that she knew better than I.

"I like reading books that correspond to my emotional state." I reminded her that I reread Thomas Hardy when winter's gray settled in. "I'm in a dark and terrifying place. I need to read a book written by someone who's been here before me."

She and I had relied on Bob for wise counsel and large love. Where was he when we needed him? He would be able to guide us through grief, help me through depression. It was odd how often each of us had the urge to call and ask him how to cope.

Rebecca had said that even in his absence she felt guided by him. Would she rather have him here where he belonged? Of course. She missed and longed for him everyday, but she also sensed his presence.

I walked Hugo home and began to read Solomon's book.

Tuesday came! The holiday ended and I made an appointment with one of Bob's colleagues. He agreed to see me that day and I felt better the minute I sat across from him.

"Don't mistake my happiness to see you for happiness," I said. "I'm depressed."

I told the story. He commiserated. "Of course," said he. "This was a weekend you and Bob especially enjoyed as you prepared for your exodus to the boat." He gave me a pill. He gave me two pills. It was a cocktail party with a good bartender.

And then the bad news. "Unfortunately, these can take six weeks to work."

Six weeks? What kind of cure was that?

"You'll feel better after Labor Day."

I always felt better after Labor Day. A hold-over from childhood. New school shoes! New lunch box! New thermos! New pencil case! When Bob went into his despond upon our return from summer vacation, I became euphoric. Wide open spaces for new beginnings. No more close quarters. No more of that intense togetherness Bob preferred. Once off the boat, the apartment seemed a wonderland. Rugs! Bookshelves! Refrigerator! I rejoiced the first day he went back to work, out the door in a suit, shoes and socks. Space. Order. Routine. No more days controlled by the whimsy of winds. For me, this was when the New Year began, not when the calendar flipped to January 1.

Labor Day was a long way off.

I made another appointment for later in the week. I needed Labor Day to cast out a line and pull me steadily towards it.

As I got up to leave, he told me, "Many of your husband's patients found their way to me. They all said the same thing. They had given up trying to find another Dr. Ascher. No other psychiatrist had measured up." He shook his head, his voice grew quiet as he said, "There are no other Dr. Aschers."

Would I have been here if there were?

You'll Feel Better After Labor Day

AND I DID. FEEL BETTER. With time, there were longer periods of feeling better. Time doesn't heal. That's nonsense. Healing is another of the great mysteries. Yes, it happens, but a lot is going on to help it happen. We begin to sew stitches over the opening of grief's pockets. We reach into them less often. With time and more stitches, fewer fingers can fit until there's only room for the pinky.

I often thought that a habit of self-sufficiency, independence and ease in solitude helped me sew the stitches. For that, I thanked my father who'd taught me as a child how to take care of myself. "Anticipate," he would say. He wanted me to know that each action had a result. I should anticipate that result and be prepared to execute, meet or avert it.

In the fourth summer, when the pockets were less deep, I rented an 18th century farmhouse in upstate New York, a thirty-minute drive from Bennington College where I was teaching. The owners had put it on the market and because they'd moved, charged nominal rent in return for my maintaining the house and keeping it ready for real estate agents' showings. The only sounds there were the wide floorboards giving to my step. There was healing and happiness. Happiness in that quiet. Happiness in nights so dark that when I walked the dog, I had to find the path to the house by the feel of the pavement's edge. There was happiness in the trout stream that ran through the property and in which I swam, floating down to the still waters beneath the covered bridge.

The first day I arrived, as I approached that bridge a few yards from the house, I saw children daring each other to jump from it while the more timid launched themselves on a rope swing from the muddy bank. For a moment I thought it was all a trick. Some Norman Rockwell, holographic tableau being played out for the New Yorker. Not so, said the local postmaster who knew everything. Rockwell had in fact painted there, riding his bike over from his nearby Vermont home. And kids really did swim there every day of summer.

By September, the house had not sold, nor did it sell for a year so I stayed on through the winter, working at an old, wooden, tavern table set up by the fire. I continued to make the weekly 3½-hour drive up from New York to spend weekends and on occasion, weeks at a time. There was peace in the wintry silence interrupted solely by the snap of a burning log, the slurp of the dog drinking from his metal bowl, the wind, and the settling of the old, weary house like someone turning over in bed to seek comfort. The resident mice moved stealthily, and I learned to outwit them before I left the house to return to New York. I piled wooden chairs on my bed to discourage their habit of making nests there.

I wrote, I taught, I edited and became peaceful with myself. Love and work. Thank you, Dr. Freud. It was true. Love of work was even truer.

And then more love than I had ever imagined, love that was so much more, so much bigger than love. How can we possibly imagine the profound that hasn't been experienced? Which is why I've yet to read anything written about grandchildren that doesn't weigh itself down with the wonder of it all. Yes, it is a wonder but no, I am not going to write about it.

Except to say that when Rebecca gave birth to twin girls nine years after Bob's death, all hands were rerquired on deck. A mother, father and grandmother to pace, rock, burp, soothe. To keep two small creatures alive. Once again, my love was directed outward with the same intensity that accompanied Bob's dying. But this time it was for life. Once again, I fell in love.

Tenth Anniversary

EVEN SO, the approach of the 10th anniversary of Bob's death brought with it an amorphous sense of dread. There had been peace. There had been ease. And now, what was this? From what dark cavern was this arising?

This is what it used to feel like when a hurricane was coming our way. As we secured the boat there would be a wary sensation between the layers of our skin. A tightening in our bellies. We worked in silence in an unnatural stillness of air. Then waited for it to hit and drag anchors across harbors to tangle with other anchors before sending the entire mess across the water to be tossed and broken on the stone jetty.

I had expected this anniversary to be pain free. I assumed I was done with grief. There was so much happiness in my life. Buck up, old girl. It's been ten years. What's the matter with you?

I consulted a cognitive therapist, a friend of Jeannette Sanger hoping he would answer that question. He said I hadn't allowed myself to grieve fully. When I reported this, Jeannette called him to protest, "Don't make her grieve more! She's done her grieving." I told him I most certainly had. I said, "As proof I should have stored the tears like pickles in a barrel."

And yet, even as I said it, I was aware that nobody grieves fully. Who could stand it? When we've found some happiness, we close the zipper on it.

The therapist urged the zipper down. Patiently. Week after week. It was stuck. He applied a therapeutic equivalent of paraffin — an insight here, an interpretation there. It slipped a notch. Two notches.

I zipped it back up one notch. "Can't you just marry me?" I asked. "That would fix everything."

He would make a good husband, thought I. So kind. So caring. We'd keep our lives as they were. I wouldn't move out nor would I allow him to move in. We'd just be married.

We both laughed at the absurdity of transference.

I fought his efforts to free me. I'd been feeling just fine, thank you until this blip on the screen.

I told him everything would be better if I changed professions and did something that required work with my hands. Something I could start and at the end of the workday, see the results. Like building chairs. Something physical. That I lacked the necessary skills didn't dissuade me.

"What a shame that on occasion you still feel this way."

And then I didn't. Feel that way.

Bob entered the consulting room. I sensed him hovering behind me as I wept for all that had been lost. "I miss him," I cried. After all these years.

Physicists have demonstrated that mere light can move particles and change everything. All it takes is the lightest touch. What I experienced was a shift of the threshold of my awareness.

Once I left the office and headed for the Columbus Avenue bus, Bob's voice, unmistakable came from behind. "I've got your back, Babe."

Cosmic Winks

YES. HE WAS CLOSE. Very, very close. Rebecca and I had sensed this with such certainty we never suffered the regret others presumed inevitable, that he hadn't lived to meet her daughters. It seemed clear that he was with and "knew" them.

Never did we think he'd left us for Titian's heaven. That destination to which the Virgin soars in The Assumption. When one enters the Frari Church in Venice catching sight of the painting, you can almost hear, the "whoosh!" as she makes her swift ascent.

Up she goes and down come the puti to lead the way. To coax, push and pull the cloud upon which she stands.

This heaven vibrates with tension between the earthly and divine, with the mind-blowing drama of their occasional intersection. God's expression suggests an admonishing, "Speed it up!" The cherubim are doing their best to oblige while below, apostles gaze upward with "wow!" expressions.

The painting's power can make us feel stuck down here, heavy with incidentals and questionings. It awakens a longing for… what? Vast love? Homecoming? A belief that what looks like "the end" is an inauguration? Andre Malraux thought, "The greatest mystery is not that we have been flung at random among the profusion of the earth and the galaxy of the stars, but that in this prison we can fashion images of ourselves sufficiently powerful to deny our nothingness." We insist on it. Titian painted it.

Titian's heaven is welcoming and action packed. A California freeway, a ski-in-ski-out resort. So many comings and goings humming with gossip.

I understand the longing to put faith in that, to affix a sacred stamp asserting, "Yes!" The sky does open and like a vacuum cleaner sucks up the righteous. But I didn't because there was too much "evidence" of Bob's being in and out of our lives depending on our awareness and lack of distraction.

Belief answers to hope. No wonder humankind is drawn to its magnetic field. We seem determined to believe in something, even if it's our own disbelief. My father's absolute certainty, "When you're dead your dead," offered him comfort, easing the discomfit of who-knows? Our minds aren't equipped for the shock of vitality snuffed out causing us to trip over the spaces they left behind. Whoops. Gone. Like so much dish water down the drain. No wonder we elevate the state of our deceased. No wonder Titian perfected heaven's memorable blue, a shade that grabs, holds onto and remains in visual memory.

So much chatter throughout history, so many words uttered in response to the ultimate, "Huh?"

We lay claim to our dead in a way impossible in their lives. We hold them within our power, moving them about like so many toy soldiers. We continue their stories where they left off, providing their endings. We pronounce their destinations with such certitude it's surprising we don't receive postcards. "Kind of boring." "Weather's great." "Wish you were here."

Gravestone engravings, shared conversations, the "In Memoriam" section of the Times Obituaries bear witness to our claims:

"Called home."

"Into the sunshine."

"Walking hand in hand with our Lord."

"Asleep in Jesus"

"He's in a far better place."

"Aunt Gladys will come back as a toad."

"Now she's with her sister."

"Sam has crossed over."

"He made his transition."

My uncle, a Born Again Christian tried one last time, while at my dying father's bedside, to bring him to Jesus. "I want to play basketball with you in heaven," he wept.

The idea of an "afterlife" is up for grabs. Why would it adhere to our architectural renderings, our limited knowledge of time and space? For Socrates it was lively. According to Plato he was in fine spirits on the day of his death, secure in his belief that having mastered the ability to see the ideal realization of temporal forms, he would be joining others who shared this mastery. Once separated from the demands, distractions, and prison of the body, they could focus on things as they were rather than as seen through the fictions created by the living.

There was a parallel in my friend Margot's statement at the age of 101 when she was comfortable with and accepting of the inevitable, "It's so precious. It means so much to leave this life and start a new one with people who know what I want." As a Buddhist she believed in reincarnation and told us, her friends, "With perseverance and extra help from teachers, we can break through this fog that is keeping us from knowing what it is like to leave this body."

The Dalai Lama has written that one of his main mentors, Kyapje Ling Rinpoche, was so advanced in his practice that he could recall past lives. "As a fully ordained monk, had Rinpoche claimed superior cognition without this being true, he would have broken his vow to abstain from false proclamation of spiritual realizations, and he would have had to disrobe!" I liked the optimism inherent in that. It made room for the possibility that we might be lucky the next time around, might get a little better at life.

Rather than being "up there," perhaps "heaven" surrounds us separated from view by our habits of looking, of seeing. Isn't it as likely that the dead are a mere finger's poke away, visible if we could pierce the veil of our unknowing?

Perhaps we would get closer to "truth" if, as suggested by physicist Alan Lightman we accepted that certain mysteries remain unanswerable. Or don't respond to our mode of inquiry. Perhaps truth exists in uncertainty. Perhaps it appears as William James suggests, in glimmers, flashes of intuition and imagination. Now we see it, now we don't. Why not trust that as did conjurers of truth Shakespeare and the Psalmists? Why not trust our own intuition? Our "visitations?" There are places the creative preconscious can go when freed of concerns about "reality," places that crack the carapace of our assumptions and preconceptions.

Do Garcia Marquez' corpses levitate? Who's to say they don't? He once commented to a mutual friend in Argentina, "Isn't it funny that in the States, they think One Hundred Years of Solitude is fiction?"

Did Bob's side of the bed levitate at night? Did "the dead want to help us," as Margot insisted? Do we on occasion hear them? Catch a glimpse of them out of the corners of our eyes? Do we discern their presence with a different kind of knowledge available to intuition and imagination?

Yes. Don't discount any of it if you agree with poet Wendell Berry who asserts, "The verb 'to imagine' contains the full richness of the verb 'to see.' It is by imagination that knowledge is 'carried to the heart'"

Bob was carried to our hearts over and over again.

It has been in moments of quiet alertness that imagination and intuition provided occasions when many of us have "seen" or "sensed" that our beloveds "appeared" as ephemerally as floaters in a middle-aged eye. Moments when a rare, quiet space bloomed in the mind and we were given a glimpse of what might be. Moments that jolted us into other awareness.

We second-guess it of course. We specialize in second guesses. Did we really see what we thought we saw? Did we construct a dream based on a fervent desire that it be so? One of the above?

None of the above? All of the above?

Many years ago, while on tour for a book about my brother, members of the audience would approach following a reading and discussion. One by one, in different bookstores in different cities, with a bit of hesitancy they would share their stories. A young woman in Chicago shyly whispered that the week after her brother died, she went to his apartment, "I was fumbling with the key outside his door and suddenly the scent of his aftershave filled the hallway." She described the air as being dense with it. She wrinkled her nose and laughed, "I never liked that scent. Aramis." When the same event occurred on her second visit, she said aloud, "Stop it!" And "he" did.

A Jesuit priest approached one night following a reading in Washington. He waited until I'd finished signing books and the manager was folding chairs and dimming the lights. He spoke in a voice so soft I wondered if he were praying. "I just saw something, this afternoon." He paused and I urged, "What was it?"

"I officiated at the burial of a young man who'd died of AIDS. His parents were so ashamed, they told no one, invited no one to the funeral, and had him buried in a cemetery far from their town." I winced. "Yes. But then, as his casket was lowered into the ground, a flock of seagulls appeared above us, landed and formed a circle around the open grave." He chuckled, "And this parents thought no one would come."

There were enough similar stories that upon my return I suggested to my editor that we might consider having my next book address these experiences. "Barbara! You're not woo-woo."

Getting more so every day.

Started getting more so when on the first anniversary of Bobby's death, a clock he'd given our mother for Christmas chimed. Nothing unusual about that except it hadn't worked for years and been long relegated to and forgotten in the attic. Even my father, Mr. WhenYou'reDeadYou'reDead smiled and shrugged.

Getting more so when following Margot's death an upside-down smile of a rainbow appeared at her regular entrance to Central Park. A group of people had gathered and stood, their heads back, staring up and uttering New Yorkers' favored expression of shocked befuddlement, "What the fuck?" Indeed, there it was. A rainbow standing on its head.

We took photographs and moved on. Later, when we'd post it on Instagram or text it to friends, we'd learn that wonder can't be caught in a lens. Nonetheless, we'll always press the shutter. Why not?

More so every day since a woman who lives on the North Shore of Long Island told me that following the death of her mother, a bird lover, a robin appeared at the kitchen window and persistently pecked at the screen. "It didn't surprise me that if she was to send me a message, it would be in the form of a bird and at the kitchen windows, a place we both feel very much at home. The robin's posture, as it flew among three of the kitchen windows, was closer to a hummingbird's, wings back, beak thrust forward in order to peck at the screen.

"The robin left gradually, staying on the back of a wrought iron chair for a day or so before leaving permanently." And then, a couple of days later, "A golden eagle appeared and stood in our back yard, as if waiting for my daughter and I to drive in. It stood there fixing its gaze on us, making sure we saw it, looking by turns regal and prehistoric, enormous, then flying first to perch briefly on the crossbar of the swing set and finally flying off.

"My mother had a very good sense of humor. I said, 'I got it with the robin!'"

Some of the many stories were accompanied by a "You might think I'm crazy" look or an "I know this can't be true" look. Can't be true but…a "but" hung in the air. I put my faith in that "but,"

I'm not an evangelist for these occurrences. When hearing or reading about such "appearances," I had more often than not sided with the unaccepting intellect. But there have been enough instances both experienced and reported that to avoid acknowledging them would be disingenuous. Make of them what you will. Make nothing of them as you will.

What I made of them was that it was time for a conversation with two friends, art historian Joel Upton and physicist Arthur Zjonc, former Amherst College professors. I'd drawn on their expertise over the years. For an earlier book, I had relied on Zjonc's scientific mind and Upton's spiritual. We made arrangements to meet in the former's office in Springfield, Massachusetts.

Following greetings, I told them about my experience with what I referred to as "Cosmic winks." Were they familiar with such moments? Zjonc speaking so quietly I had to lean in to hear him said, "These sightings occur too frequently to be coincidental." He added, "But physicists will never believe it." Spoken by one of their own. "The proof is in the experience," rather than the lab or superconductor.

He explained that we fail to believe "what we can't conceive, but the world is penetrated," by these "others." Upton nodded, "Yes. Infinity suffuses our finite life."

As we spoke, the pale, winter sun that had illuminated a Tibetan rug gave way to darkness and none of us got up to turn on a light.

I told them that a week ago as I was meditating, I thought I'd experienced such a suffusion. I "saw" golden, vibrating filaments as fine as a spider's silk spreading out and up to infinity. "The point of origin was at the bottom, as though coming from my mind." I laughed, "Well, of course it was." I reported that in that moment I knew what it was and said to myself, "So, that's what love looks like." I told them, "What was odd was that it was an all-encompassing but impersonal love."

"Yes," was Arthur's sole response. "Yes."

Oh. And then, there were the birds. Ah, yes. Once more, the birds.

In her 100th, wise and lucid year, Margot advised, "Watch for the birds." She spoke of scattering her sister's ashes in a stream "when a great blue heron appeared and flew above them as they floated away." After a moment, she added, "There have been many experiences like that."

Yes, I told her there'd been sightings that elicited the thought, "Bob" rather than "finch," or "hawk." The same had happened after my towhead brother Bobby's death. As I walked through a winter gray, German forest a flamboyant, male gold finch landed on a branch above me. It's yellow against the somber backdrop appeared almost garish, unusual in winter when they are a dull buff. "Bobby," I thought.

But, "thought" wasn't the right word. The response was far quicker and sharper than thought. It had been sudden, clear awareness followed by certainty. My bird sightings had the same effect as music; they registered in a realm outside the rational mind and inspired a sense of wonder and gratitude. Like listening to Bach.

Many years ago, on a late, sun scorched August afternoon, when we were sailing far offshore, a yellow warbler flew into the cockpit and perched on Bob's bare foot. "Come here!" He whispered, urging me up from the cabin. He pointed down and we both stared remaining as still and silent as the bird that stayed for at least an hour until once more taking flight. "Maybe it's migrating and needed a rest," I suggested. Sometimes there are no words. I was to learn that there are many such times and that it was important not to rush in with my "explanations" or quick dismissals. There are experiences not well served by language.

The other day, a yellow warbler huddled in a planter on my terrace, the first time I'd ever witnessed such a thing. Perhaps it too needed a rest. I put down water and left it alone other than to check on it through the afternoon and before I went to sleep that night. By morning, it had flown away.

It is as rare for a warbler to rest on a bare foot at sea or in a pot on a New York City terrace as it is for hawks to appear with the frequency they did for my daughter. Forthright, no-nonsense, intelligent she nonetheless knew that the red-tailed hawk flying over her head and occasionally perching on branches just ahead of her during her daily runs through Central Park was in some form, an appearance of her father. Bob was an enthusiastic hawk watcher in life and now he was "showing up" as the bird.

Rebecca was not a birder. She knew her robins, cardinals, sparrows and blue jays. Unlike her father, she didn't go looking for red-tailed hawks and yet, they kept showing up wherever she was — in places as unlikely as a tollbooth on the JFK Bridge as she passed through. They circled her house in the country. They flew past the window of her city apartment. They appeared in the playground where she took her children and where one swooped so low the other day that it caused a seasoned, Manhattan mother to crouch down and shelter her child's head with her arms. "Holy shit!"

"It's just Mom's hawk," her five-year-old daughters reassured.

Many years before Bob died, one of his colleagues with whom we were dining began to tell a story in the same matter of fact tone in which the two men had been discussing borderline personality disorder.

The previous weekend, he and his wife were in the Berkshires to attend a friend's memorial service in a small, country church. The young woman had died of cancer leaving behind a two-year-old daughter who sat in the front pew next to her father. "The window was open because it was a warm day and a small bird flew through it, circled the child's head and flew out again. Everybody saw it. Everybody 'knew.'"

Yes, they happen, these cosmic winks — Rebecca's hawk, the bird flying around a little girl's head, Bobby's clock.

Perhaps the music Bob heard in Venice was a nudge prompting him to say that being there "makes it o.k. to die."

In the last five years of Bob's life, one of his toes crossed the other and each day before putting on his shoes he wrapped it in lamb's wool. One of Rebecca and Chuck's newborn twins' toes sat atop another. The same toe. Rebecca and I stared. We laughed. A Cosmic wink.

The pediatrician said, "It will straighten out. That's just the way it was in the womb." Rebecca and I knew it wouldn't. Yes, he was here. The universe chuckled.

A Heron

OF COURSE, THAT IS WHEN IT HAPPENS.

When there is love and work. When longing has given way to fulfillment, sorrow to delight. When life feels just right, thank you.

I had achieved long fought for contentment, a bland, drab word you wouldn't invite to a dance. A word like "O.K" or "satisfaction" (minus the Stones.)

There are times when we want our lives to be a little bit, wow! A little bit Marvel comic. But I'd had it with the "ZAP!" the "EEYOW," the "BOING!" and the "BLAP!" I preferred this refuge from an exclamation point littered landscape.

Unlike the speaker in Wallace Stevens, "Sunday Morning," "in contentment" I did not "feel/the need of some imperishable bliss." I'd had more than my share of bliss and it had perished. What else was it going to do?

I preferred contentment's quiet steadiness requiring nothing more than itself and my guardianship. I held a treasure chest. Independence. Silence in solitude. Family, friends, profession, a roof over my head, food on the table.

In contentment, the heart no longer hungers. It has none of the sharp angles and edges of happiness. Its contours are softer. In time, when a border collie would come into my life, I'd watch the quiet way he strolled into the bay until the water held him and feathered his fur to either side reminding me of a floating woman in a skirted bathing suit. No splash, no purpose, no wild fetching of a ball or stick, just slow emersion and forward motion. Contentment.

Happiness, its close cousin is full of splash and purpose, the purpose being to cling to itself and watch its back. Contentment lacks the clinging that arises from the fear that it will end, be taken away.

So, the irony of it. The nerve! When there is no more need, an unknown need emits its signal decipherable only by dogs and children no larger than dogs.

Just when you wouldn't change a thing, change asserts and insists. Little wonder we hate it and its bossy ways.

It invades contentment, takes it by the shoulders and shakes. I looked away and stood my ground, the quiet steady ground of my Goldberg Variations emotional state.

Wouldn't you know, in late August a visitor arrived. A man on whom I'd had a harmless crush since being seated next to him three years previously at a dinner in Washington at the Swedish Embassy. We had shared the information strangers share, making conversation and hoping for a story, perhaps a connection, something more than the perfunctory formalities engaged in at such events. We spoke about our education, our interests, our late spouses. I had studied English Literature, "And you?" "Russian."

The conversation ended as he gathered his notes and stood to deliver a speech.

At the end of the evening, when he, as the host stood at the door bidding people goodnight, I stopped to ask, "Why Russian?"

"Because in school I fell in love with the Russian lyric poets and wanted to read them in the original." I didn't exactly swoon but...

We began an email correspondence initiated by my asking which of those poets were his favorites? Could he recommend a translation? No, there were no adequate translations. "Except for Nabokov's and that's almost impossible to come by." A month later, a tattered book arrived, Nabokov's. With a note, "I'm sorry, this is the best I could find."

It had been six years since his wife's death and he was an attractive, intelligent man with a reputation for integrity and kindness in

Washington, a town with more single women than single men. I presumed he'd remarried or had a live-in partner.

We continued to correspond about poetry, saw each other at meetings a few times a year and during a group trip to Austria. I had gotten the vague outlines. Articulate, gracious, my preferred body type.

"You'll always be attracted to..." The tweedy man in Chicago.

By this August afternoon, we were sufficiently comfortable and familiar with each other that when I learned he and Kim Churches, the Managing Director of the think tank of which he was President were scheduled to come to Long Island to present an event for the organization's major donors, I invited them to stay with me in my rented shack. Modest, not very comfortable, I warned but I could offer a laid-back community, my family who lived nearby and meals of vegetables from their garden, eggs from my grand-daughters' hens. It would be an antidote to the manicured lawns and inhabitants of Southampton where they were to appear.

Many phoned and emailed protests. They couldn't accept. It would be an imposition. "I wouldn't have invited you if I didn't think it would be fun."

They arrived and dropped their suitcases in the assigned rooms — his downstairs, hers upstairs next to mine. "Downstairs is the boys' dorm. Upstairs is the girls'."

Would they like to go for a swim? Kim declined. She had to catch up on work. So, the two of us walked to my favorite swimming spot three minutes down a road travelled by more cyclists and pedestrians than automobiles. When we arrived, there it was.

I'd been looking for a great blue heron all summer. Among Bob's and my favorite birds, I'd kept a sharp eye and become concerned when none showed up. But there it was at last, standing on one leg at the edge of the harbor.

To the heron I "said" in the same way I'd been "speaking" to Bob since he died, speaking in silence, connecting mind to mind, "O.K.

I'll pay attention." I somehow "knew" that was what I was to do. I sensed his and Margot's presence. That unquestionable change of energy, something invisible yet known entering the space.

The connection to Margot was through the story she'd told of the blue heron flying above her sister's ashes, her resulting exhortation, "Watch for the birds." Where Bob was concerned, this bird had always reminded me of him. The long, skinny legs. The wingspan. The patient, hovering, attention he brought to sailing and his practice. The sharply focused eye, the quick, darting catch of an insight, feeling most "at home" on water. "You were clearly one in your former life," I used to tell him. "Or you're on your way to becoming one."

I said none of this as I lead my guest into the water and set out for the opposite shore. We spoke of Einstein. Oh, yes. Very elevated while afloat, talking to the sky, doing the backstroke. I was showing off. We'd both read Walter Isaacson's biography and based on that, discussed relativity, reality, the concept of a unified field theory, as if I understood anything about it. "Let's go back for a glass of wine."

For the five nights of his stay our conversations ranged late and long as we sat on the deck with our feet propped against the railing. We spoke of shared passions, music and poetry. We talked about what we wanted out of life. Like kids late at night sitting on the floors of dormitory halls.

"Mom! You're in love," my daughter said when on the third night of his visit she invited us for dinner.

"Nonsense."

"Mom, I recognize that plate."

I looked down at the one I'd brought into the kitchen while clearing the table. Nothing had been eaten.

"I was too engrossed in the conversation."

"Yeah, right."

Yeah, she was right.

We continued to return to the same swimming spot late each day when the sun was low over the water. I spoke of my mother's recent death and he of his beloved father's a few months earlier. We spoke of our beloved, missing and missed spouses. The difference between us was that he "hated being a widower," whereas I relished my single life. "I'm not looking for trouble," I said.

He later told me that he'd responded, "I'm looking for trouble." My ears must have been under water.

The heron didn't reappear until our last evening swim before my guest's return to Washington. There it was, in the same spot. Tall, still and profound.

I regarded it worthy of attention, this framing of arrival and departure. And I took it as a "sign," mystery's way of tapping us out of our sleepiness, urging, "Pay attention."

The next morning after packing and putting his luggage in the car, he suggested one more walk on the ocean beach where we'd taken the dog each day. Fine. We threw a tennis ball. We picked up poop. We were quiet until he made what he called his "declaration of certainty." He loved me and wanted me in his life. Forever. My knees went ridiculously weak.

"Do you mind if we sit down?" He told me he believed in romantic love. He told me that he'd thought that part of his life had died with his wife, but he'd been wrong. He'd had a secret dream, "secret even from myself. But here you are…"

I thought, "But we haven't even kissed!" And said, "If I were the person I was soon after Bob died, I would now say to you, 'Let's go to Ashawagh Hall and get married.'" The Hall, a former 1847 schoolhouse on the village green of our hamlet was now used for community events, not weddings. It didn't matter. That's what I blurted out in this moment of astonishment. And then added, "But, I'm no longer that person and so, I'd like you to return to Washington and your regular life and think about all of this." I didn't know yet that this was a man who didn't speak until he'd thought a great deal about the words that would come out of his mouth. He'd tested them for truth and certainty.

These five days had been magical. The knitting together of a bond and something bigger. The revelation of what had been going on for three years but which we'd been too dense to see. Would this professed love stand up to the demands of the work-a-day world? I wasn't sure. There had been nothing work-a-day about our time together. The last night, we had burst into song. Sitting in the dark after dinner, for no apparent reason, we began singing Broadway show tunes. Yes, those songs. His parents, as my own, went to New York once a year to see musicals, bringing back the albums to share with the family.

We shouted out, "When you see a guy…" "What's playing at the Roxy…" "I'll know when my love comes along…" He sang the Sky Masterson part, "And you'll know at a glance, by the two pair of pants." And I, Sister Sarah, "Yes, I'll know…"

On to South Pacific and The King and I. His momentary concern about "waking up the neighbors" was met by more song. Here was unsteady on its feet, knock-kneed happiness.

Now, as we stood up to leave the beach and head for the Jitney, two swans flew above our heads.

"Wow," I pointed.

Speaking of his father he said, "Swans were Bud's favorite birds."

I remained silent about the only other time two swans had flown over my head.

When he called the next day he said, "I had the strangest dream. There was a great blue heron perched on Ashawagh Hall's weathervane."

Entreaties

LONG, LATE NIGHT CALLS in the ensuing weeks ended only with our cell phone batteries. He wrote love poems and letters. He continued to press his suit.

And I continued to be grateful and in love and to protest against commitment. No matter that what was happening felt, well... cliché, cliché, cliché... miraculous. I stood on its border wondering for the second time in my life, what were the chances?

I'd long ago accepted that nobody gets a second chance. That few get a first. I'd had my turn. So, why this?

He ignored the hand I held up to stay him, to stay fate. He remained clear that one does not turn away from the gift we'd been given. He was certain of his love and wanted to marry me. I suggested, "Why can't we just be lovers?" I didn't need marriage to dive into this unexpected, unasked for second astonishment, this opportunity to learn more about love and perhaps learn to be better at it.

To say, yes would require spending less time with friends and family I held dear in this city that had been home my entire adult life. This city with its cacophony of "Fuck you," its theaters crackling with lozenge wrappers, its streets resonating with the staccato of honking cabs, the babble of children tumbling out of school into the park and the squeak, squeak, squeak of dueling swing chains, its "excuse-me-I-was-in-line-ahead of you," its "Don't-give-me-a-parking-ticket-I'm-almost there..." its "Asshole!" Music to my ears. Home gritty home.

Gone would be the daily in and out of granddaughters' lives

— walks to school, evening stories, kiss, kiss, hug, hug, tuck into bed. No. That would be too wrenching. No. To say, yes would complicate a life made simple by the sharpening of focus, the slow, persistent shedding of the superfluous, a lighter way of moving across the remaining landscape, something that comes with age, the narrowing of time, the shedding of sorrow.

My protests were met with, "I believe in the sanctity of marriage," and, "Marriage is an honorable institution." Yes, he said that, this fine, handsome, smart, funny, sexy, fascinating, old-fashioned, courtly man who seemed to have left his heart in the 19th century.

Over the weeks, my resistance began to waver as I kept hearing Bob's insistence in life that, "Love begets more love."

I was in an embarrassing state. Sixteen years old, not sixty-nine in love. I couldn't sleep, I couldn't concentrate, I couldn't eat. Kevin Abernathy fed me daily BLT's, the one food I could manage. She and I would join in the hilarity of fantasy weddings. Fantasy weddings that didn't upend my life.

I waited for the phone to ring. I ran to report to Rebecca that he'd called to say we'd forgotten to sing one song. I'd asked which. He wanted me to think harder I couldn't come up with it. "Younger Than Springtime," he'd said. Crouching next to my daughter on the beach, in the telling, I actually uttered the exclamatory, "Oh, My God!"

He worked to persuade, I deflected the seduction of his sincerity, the reasonableness of his arguments. He suggested I come for a visit. "I think it's time for your dog to meet my dogs." Whoa! Now it was getting serious. He drove five hours to pick us up, arriving at 7 in the morning. Upon arrival in D.C., he showed me to the guest room with its single bed. Huh?

My dog met his dogs. His family met me. I learned more about him, he was a classical guitarist too shy to play for an audience even if it was only one person. So, I crouched behind a chair to listen to him practice Vivaldi's Largo. So much passion flowing into those strings. We went for walks, out to dinner, and talked with ongoing ease and sense of timelessness. He read aloud to me from Dante's *Paradisio*. He read Yeat's, "When You are Old and Gray," and his voice caught. How could it not? His wife had died without having a chance to grow old. "You don't have to do this," I said. "I want to." He continued, "But one man loved the pilgrim soul in you."

At the end of the weekend, before we'd driven down to the end of driveway, he looked at me and asked, "When do you want to do this?"

"Do what?"

"Get married?"

"Is that a proposal?"

"Only my fourth."

In spite of everything, this seemed sudden. At a loss for a response, I treaded the water of the conversation and asked, "When do you want to get married?"

"Thursday."

By the time he'd dropped me off in the City, by the time he'd driven back to D.C., by the time we'd had another late-night call, I began to relent because this was what the man I loved wanted. Believed in. I did so with the proviso to split my time between the two cities, the only way fair to my grandchildren and my work. I relented because I also heard Bob's not infrequent reminder that "the greatest testament to our love would be for you to fall in love and marry again." I relented because Bob had taught me that love was an ongoing stream growing on itself and flowing through life. Each love was a conglomeration of all our loves.

He would have answered the riddle differently. If asked, "What's at the end of a great love affair?" He would have said, "There is no end. It lives on in the next."

"Don't take your wedding ring off," I urged when I agreed to marriage. "Add mine to it."

With a return trip to Long Island for a weekend with Chuck, Rebecca, the girls and me, he asked permission for my "hand." (Now, there's an odd one.) Rebecca responded, "Phew! Over to you!" He invited my five-year-old granddaughters to walk with him on the beach. "Can Baba come?" Of course, I would.

As we walked, he spoke in a tone absent the goopy way adults address children as though children don't know that grownups don't speak like that to other grownups. "I want to marry your grandmother. What do you think of that?" "Fine," one said and ran back to friends she'd spotted on the beach. Not so fine, I thought. Watch that one.

The other, still holding my hand, looked down at her feet and mumbled, "I'm not sure it's fine." Strobe left us alone when I suggested she and I sit down and talk about it.

"So sweety, would you like to tell me why it's not fine?"

There was silence before the tears. "Because I want to marry you."

I put my arms around her, "We've been married for a long, long time and will be married for a long, long time." I believed it.

It wasn't "so fine," for his children either. Too soon. They didn't trust the apparent speed with which he'd fallen in love.

And anyway, they had other potential spouses in mind.

My former beau forsaken for this man was an acquaintance of one of the sons and called with vengeful, dire fictions about me. Nothing worse than what he was spreading around the city causing friends' gallant husbands to offer show downs in defense of my honor. They'd cancel his membership in their clubs. Gunfight at the Knickerbocker Corral. Sweet, funny and declined. He needed his false story. What else is a man scorned to do with his fury other than hide shame behind righteous outrage?

"The family needs more emotional foreplay," according to a senior member of his. To which a friend of Rebecca's replied, "You two know that the earth can open up beneath your feet at any time, so get on with it."

We allowed five months of "emotional foreplay." You can pet just so long in the back seat of a car. Then it's time to get behind the wheel.

Vows

AND SO, THERE I WAS, listing between my stepson and son-in-law who held tight as they marched me towards the man waiting by our makeshift altar in the stately, wood paneled reading room of the New York Society Library. This was where I'd been reading and writing since college. This was where I sat on the floor reading to my granddaughters. And it was here that Rebecca pointed to and read her first word. "Cat!" We had stared at each other in wonder, and I told her, "An entire world just opened up for you!"

And a new one was opening for me as I linked arms with Steve and Chuck who propelled me forward. "When we get there, don't let go," I whispered. "I am going to let go and a good man is going to hold you," said Steve who had met this good man when I took him to Cambridge to meet "my steps." No pressure but, "If they don't like you, it's a deal breaker." They liked him. They were crazy about him. They told me I'd be nuts not to marry him.

These two men I loved who steadied my progress were not turning back, were going to let go. They knew this was as it should be. I heard Bob's instructions for alleviating seasickness, "Keep your eyes on the horizon."

Of course, my knees shook. Anybody with her wits about her would tremble with the certain knowledge that the likely ending of this love story was that one of us would be left weeping at the grave, in love with a ghost. And yet, I continued towards the ruthless, radical contract we were about to enter.

There had been no trembling the first time around, no holding back, none of this calling upon courage. When I was young and new to love and the resulting marriage, when I recited the vows, I focused on "love and cherish." Yes, yes, yes! I will, I will! I slid over the words "'till death us do part." How can the young know? It's not as though these astonishing vows romanticize what they demand of us. No, we do that all by ourselves.

Not so this time around. Now we both knew more about the enormity of love, how it stretched to infinity. Now we knew what it exacted of us.

Who can explain what makes us risk so much in order to be joined by love? The man towards whom I walked could. He had been without doubt. He told our families and friends that because each of us had been blessed with long, love-filled marriages, "We want more." How else to honor what we had had then and what we had now? What else to do with this consuming joy?

Yes, there was that. And there was mystery that moved him to open his arms and me to proceed toward them to declare, "until death us do part."

ACKNOWLEDGMENTS

THANK YOU TO THOSE WHO BROUGHT ME FROM THERE TO HERE: Tshering Lama, Kevin and Jim Abernathy, Jeannette and Alex Sanger, Carolyn and Ian Mackenzie, Jennifer Brown and Paul Simon, Becky Okrent, Laura Palmer, Darina Byrne, Gary Rosenberg, Stuart Seidman, Symra Cohn, the Tea Ladies and Margot's Thursday Group.

Thank you, Nancy Newhouse and Lily Tuck for taking me into your homes when I was without one.

Early readers Jane Rosenman, Joan Hardy Clark, Maggie Goodlander and Lynn Goldberg improved this book with their keen assessments.

My Two Wise Men from the East, Joel Upton and Arthur Zajonc were essential to this book as they were to the previous one.

Without Bill Clinton's sagacious encouragement this book might not have been finished.

I am grateful to the New York Society Library for providing a writers' room and brilliant staff, especially Steve McQuirl, Head of Acquisitions and Assistant Head, Patrick Rayner who somehow know just the book in the stacks that will shed light on my subject, whatever that might be.

Thank you, Stephen and Joanna Breyer, Victoria Nuland and Robert Kagan, Emily and Antoine van Agtmael, Wanda Rapaczynski, Jessie and Robert Einhorn, Meena and Liaguat Ahamed, Marjo Talbott and Mark Vershbow for keeping Strobe well fed and in good company in D.C. while I was holed up in the above library in NYC.

It was a stroke of greatest good fortune (something to do with bees and honey) that my manuscript fell into the hands of a man

I'd admired since he published the first annual anthology, *Pushcart Prize; Best of the Small Presses*. Bill Henderson's contribution to literature is legion; to have him as my editor and publisher has been a great honor.

Elizabeth, Ellen, and Steven Ascher and families, Rebecca and Chuck Ascher-Walsh, your love makes all the difference.

Dahlia and Athena Ascher-Walsh thank you for bringing me joy. And dear Strobe, thank you for your goodness.